Whiskey
MAKERS IN
WASHINGTON, D.C.

Whiskey
MAKERS IN
WASHINGTON, D.C.

A
PRE-PROHIBITION
HISTORY

TROY HUGHES

THE
History
PRESS

Published by The History Press
Charleston, SC
www.historypress.com

First published 2023

Manufactured in the United States

ISBN 9781467153379

Library of Congress Control Number: 2022947091

People who drank the old-time whiskey did not have stomachs disordered as they do now from drinking rectified whiskey. An old whiskey is the better and healthier. Before the introduction of whiskey made from high wines or rectified cologne spirits, with oils and flavoring extracts, a man never had the jimjams. He never drank to excess; his wife allowed him to stay at home. One drink did not create a thirst for another. The average man did not get drunk.

—straight whiskey lobbyist, 1906

CONTENTS

Preface   9
Acknowledgements   13

PART 1: A BIT OF AMERICAN WHISKEY HISTORY
1. Why Rye?   16
2. The Alcohol Tax   19
3. The Rise of the Rectifiers   23
4. The War to Define What Whiskey Is   28
5. Sons of Temperance   58

PART II: THE WHISKEY PRODUCERS
6. William D. Barry: Mount Pleasant Club Whiskey   70
7. John R. Morris: Westover Rye   89
8. James Charles McGuire: Federal Seal Rye Whiskey   96
9. Charles Kraemer: Fineza Rye   102
10. Patrick J. Drury: Haviland Rye Whiskey   112
11. Christian Xander: Old Reserve Rye   115
12. William Muehleisen Sr.: Oakmont Rye   123
13. James Tharp: Berkeley Pure Rye   126
14. William J. Donovan: Columbia Club   133

Epilogue   159
Bibliography   161
Index   171
About the Author   175

PREFACE

This book is one of two outgrowths from a gift given to me by the previous owner of my house in the Mount Pleasant neighborhood of Washington, D.C. The gift was an empty 110-year-old whiskey bottle with its label still on it. After longingly looking at the bottle as it sat on my home office desk during the first COVID winter, I made the decision to create a T-shirt that incorporated the label's design on the front and the embossed characters on the back as a sort of neighborhood pride effort. I figured I needed to give the shirt some sort of historical context, so I dug into finding out as much as I could about the guy whose name appears on the bottle and his store: William D. Barry, Reliable Family Liquor Store. This initial research led to what would later become this book. It turns out that Barry wasn't just a liquor store owner; he was also a leader in the fight to keep the District "wet" as the temperance forces slowly gained strength in the early 1900s.

The label's "Recommended by Physicians" and "Vatted and Blended" text also made me curious. In researching the explanations for these blurbs, I stumbled on a whole world of interesting (to me, at least) legislative and judicial fights on how whiskey came to be regulated and taxed by the federal government. The fight to sway the public's opinion on the question "What is whiskey?" in the advertisements and in all three branches of government took over ten years to resolve.

Learning about the life and times of Barry's fellow liquor merchants (some of whom lived right here in Mount Pleasant, which, at the time, was

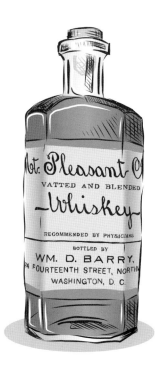

An artist's rendition of Mount Pleasant Club Whiskey bottle. *Christina Owens Knapp.*

a very dry suburb of the city) provided an excellent backdrop for this book—a sort of time capsule for understanding what the District used to look like. All the seeming disparate topics that are covered, from the use of racial restrictive covenants to keep Black Americans out of the neighborhood to the guy in the pocket of the straight whiskey producers who later became the father of the Food and Drug Administration, the quasi-Masonic secret temperance society and the Senators and the tragic tale of one of the team's stars who liked whiskey a bit too much, all somehow connect back to these early whiskey makers.

The neighborhood loved the T-shirts, and it spawned in me the crazy idea to try to revive the long-dead brand "Mount Pleasant Club Whiskey." With my friend and neighbor, John Loughner, we did just that with our company Reboot Beverages, LLC. So, like the men I write about in this book, I, too, am now a whiskey producer. And also like them (spoiler alert), I am what is today known as a non-distilling producer—we don't distill our own liquors, and neither did any of the pre-Prohibition distillers who are covered in the book. They, for the most part, got their whiskeys from neighboring Maryland, which punched way above its weight in the whiskey production world (especially with its rye) prior to Prohibition. Uncovering these producers' old advertisements, along with some of the gimmicks they employed to promote their products (some reproduced here), was simply fascinating to me as someone who is now in the business of trying to sell booze to John Q. Public.

TO E OR NOT TO E: IS IT WHISKEY OR WHISKY?

Before we get started, I need to address this issue. In general terms, either spelling is an umbrella term for a type of distilled spirit made from a mash of fermented grains. The modern rule of thumb is:

- Countries that have Es in their name (the United States and Ireland, for example) tend to use *whiskey* (plural, *whiskeys*).

- Countries without Es in their name (Canada, Scotland and Japan, for example) use *whisky* (plural *whiskies*).

In this book, I will default to using the E, but as you will see, the newspapers and advertisements prior to Prohibition alternated the spelling with no discernable rhyme or reason.

ACKNOWLEDGEMENTS

*M*y thanks go out to so many who helped make this book possible. First and foremost, I'd like to thank Noel Gessner, who graciously gifted me the whiskey bottle that started all of this. Next is John Loughner, who is my partner in crime when wading through this world of liquor. My friend Gina Keeney is up next; she is a researcher extraordinaire who uncovered many obscure details and wonderful stories that are recounted here. When I reached out to Mara Cherkasky, the historian who literally wrote the book on the neighborhood's history, she encouraged me to move forward when I told her I was going to try my hand at writing a book. Thanks to my neighbors who loaned me their precious whiskey bottles: Greg Lavallee (Federal Seal), Deirdre Warner-Kramer (Haviland Rye) and Scott Cartwright, who brought to my attention his pieces of a bottle of Westover Rye. A special thanks goes to Christina Owens Knapp of HellowYellow, who provided the most excellent line drawings of the bottles, and to my friend Jason Hamacher, who photographed the bottles. I didn't know what to expect when William Barry's great-grandson reached out to us. I was pleasantly surprised. Thank you, Ray Barry, for your pictures and personal insights of Mr. Barry. Kate Jenkins, my acquisition editor, thank you for holding my first-time author hand and getting me through the initial steps of the publication process. Rick Reinhard, thank you for the cool author photograph you took before Reboot's first anniversary shindig. And finally, thanks to my wife, Toni Harmer, for giving me the time and space to embark on these endeavors.

PART I

A BIT OF AMERICAN WHISKEY HISTORY

1

WHY RYE?

*I*t is not a coincidence that each of the pre-Prohibition liquor merchants who are the focus of this book had rye whiskey as their flagship brand. In the time between the Revolutionary War and Prohibition, the rye style of whiskey was the most popular in the mid-Atlantic states. Prior to the Revolution, rum was the spirit of choice for the colonies and was imported from and made from molasses from the Caribbean. When the British blockaded American ports, the imports of rum and molasses were cut off, forcing thirsty colonists to elevate whiskey as their drink of choice. Whiskey had been distilled in the colonies from the beginning. The first license issued to a distiller in America was given on April 30, 1652, by the Virginia legislature:

> *It is ordered that Mr. George Fletcher shall have to himself, his heirs, ex'rs. And adm'rs. Liberty to distill and brew in wooden vessels which none have experience in but himself for 14 years, and it is further ordered that no person or persons whatsoever shall make use thereof within this colony without agreeing with the said Mr. Fletcher under the penalty of 100-pound sterl.*

The compounding of spirits (mixing two separate spirits into one), that is, the art of the rectifier seems to have been objectionable from the very start. The Virginia legislature met in November 1645 and passed the following:

WHEREAS there has been great abuse by the unreasonable rates exacted by ordinary keepers, and retailers of wine and strong waters, be it enacted *that no person or persons whatsoever retailing wines or strong waters shall exact or take for any…English strong waters above the rate of 80lb. of tobacco per gall. And for aqua vitae or brandy above the rate of 40 lb. tob'o. per gallon.*

And if any person or persons retaileing [sic] *wines or strong waters as aforesaid shall fraudulently mix or corrupt the same, Upon complaint and due proofe made thereof before tow commissioners whereof one to be of the quorum, The said commissioners shall by warrant under their hands command the constables to stave the same, and if any shall take more than such rates set they to be fined at double the value of such rates soe exacted.*

The grain rye, known by its species *Secale cereale*, was the most prevalent in colonial America. It was known to be easier to grow and hardier than barley. Rye grew in bad soil conditions; it could tolerate too little or too much rain and could withstand a frost. Scotch-Irish settlers in Maryland and German Scottish settlers in Pennsylvania made beer, bread and whiskey from rye in their small farm stills. Wheat was more finicky and harder to grow, and the corn was still new to the settlers and was more prominent below the Mason-Dixon line.

Two distinct styles of rye whiskey were developed during the colonial era, known as the Maryland and Pennsylvania styles. The Pennsylvania rye style, also known as Monongahela rye (named after the river valley that gave the region in western Pennsylvania its name), commonly had a mash bill that was made up of almost all rye with just small amounts of malted barley and corn. This high rye content led to a full-bodied, sharp and spicy taste. The first whiskey brand name filed with the U.S. Trademark Registry was Pennsylvania's A. Overholt and Co. Pure Rye in 1810. The name Monongahela being associated with rye earned a cache in advertising and commanded a premium, akin to adding "Highland" to a scotch today. With more corn in its mash bill, Maryland rye was much more mellow than its sibling from the north. As for the actual taste, a whiskey expert stated that it had "[a] hint of bitterness….[It was] spicy, a little oily, almost peppermint."

Rye whiskey flourished when the center of population remained east of the Appalachian Mountains (between the Civil War and Prohibition). Two main reasons for this fact are: (1) during the Civil War, there were many thousands of Union troops from all over the country who were garrisoned in or around the District, gave the local whiskey a try and liked it and requested it when they returned to their homes (and thanks to advances in freight rail, the Maryland producers could more easily satisfy the demand); and (2) bourbon, though produced in Kentucky during this time, hadn't yet assumed its prominence as America's drink of choice due to the fact that the only major shipping routes from Kentucky were down the Mississippi River to New Orleans or overland through the mountains. In 1886, there were seventeen states where rye whiskey was produced, and tiny Maryland ranked third nationally for whiskey production between 1881 and 1913, ranking behind only Kentucky and Pennsylvania each of those years.

In 1911, there were forty-four distilleries operating in Maryland, about half of them within the city limits of Baltimore. This had been the case for a while, as J. Thomas Scharf asserted in his 1881 book, *History of Baltimore City and County*: "The rye whiskies of Baltimore have, for years, been appreciated all over the country, and many brands are so well known as to be preferred beyond all others." In western Maryland, many of the distilleries sold their entire outputs to city rectifiers and wholesalers. Given the fact that there were no distilleries of consequence operating in the District, one may assume that most of the rye whiskeys sold in Washington, D.C., likely came from the nearby distilleries, rectifiers and wholesalers in Maryland.

2

THE ALCOHOL TAX

*T*he first tax on alcohol came as a result of the newly formed federal government's attempt to pay down the national debt of $54 million from the Revolutionary War. Passed on March 3, 1791, the tax rates were based on the strength of the product, and there was also an annual tax levied on each still. Every door of a building containing a still had to be marked with "Distiller of Spirits." In 1794, the government enacted the first occupational tax, imposed on retail dealers in wines or foreign spirits at $5 per year. These taxes remained in effect until 1802 and led to what was known as the Whiskey Rebellion, in which the small farmers/distillers of Pennsylvania, Virginia, Maryland and New York questioned the new government's power to impose such a heavy tax and, in a few instances, openly revolted against the attempts by revenue agents to collect the taxes.

At this time, there was no record of mixing whiskeys with flavors, essences, extracts or other substances. It appears that all such spirits went directly to consumers in small batches. This freshly distilled whiskey did not spend much time in barrels. These small local operations could handle the initial demand for whiskey in East Coast cities like New York, Baltimore and Philadelphia, and the time it took to get barrels from the farms to the cities was roughly ten days. Over time (around 1830), as demand increased, whiskey production moved farther west on the other side of the Alleghany Mountains, and as a consequence, the whiskey spent more time in barrels while it traveled back east. Subject to the vagaries of distance, weather and tricky, muddy mountain passes, the previously unaged whiskey now spent months in barrels where it would pick up the scents of vanilla and caramel and the reddish-brown color from the staves that we now associate with whiskey. This was an unintentional effect, but soon, customers began to enjoy this new "red-colored" whiskey and began to ask for it. Monongahela whiskey became associated with this red color. This was happening in other regions for the same reasons, as whiskey had to travel farther down rivers and over roads to get to urban areas.

This style of whiskey became wildly popular, and distillers began to store their whiskey in the same way, using new charred oak barrels (cooperage), to achieve the same effect. In addition to improving the flavor of the liquid, the barrels also, over time, removed some of the less desirable congeners (impurities) from the whiskey. This style of whiskey became known as "straight" whiskey. Over time, it became the standard for whiskey to be kept in charred oak barrels for four years to reach the proper flavoring and coloring. One of the results of aging whiskey in barrels was that harsh and unpleasant tastes from congeners, which it has when it first comes out of the still, were softened and mellowed in such a way that the flavor greatly improved.

ANOTHER WAR, ANOTHER TAX

The alcohol taxes were again instituted in 1812 to help fund the government's effort during the War of 1812. This time, in 1813, an occupational tax on retailers in wines and various liquors was introduced. These taxes were repealed in 1817. Congress turned to taxing alcohol again to help pay for the Civil War in 1862. At first, the tax was twenty cents per proof gallon (one gallon at one hundred proof or 50 percent alcohol by volume), but by 1865, it was two dollars per gallon (approximately thirty-six dollars in 2022). The tax was paid on the spirits as soon as they were produced. Given that the whiskey needed to age for a number of years before it was palatable, the tax was seen as unfair. Making distillers pay the tax up front delayed their profit from the sale. This, coupled with the fact that a certain portion of the whiskey simply disappeared—thanks, in part, to absorption and evaporation (about three gallons per barrel) over time while aging in a barrel—made distillers call for some relief. They didn't want to pay taxes up front on a product that they couldn't sell until years later, and they also didn't want to pay tax on a certain amount of liquid that they knew was going to disappear.

The solution Congress landed on was to allow for a "bonding" period of up to one year, during which the whiskey could age without being taxed. The whiskey was put into a government supervised "bonded" warehouse under the supervision of an agent known as the gauger. During the bonding period, gaugers guarded the warehouse, kept track of how long barrels had been aging, measured the contents of the barrels and administered the tax. In order to get whiskey out of the bonded warehouse, the tax had to be paid—no matter what. In the case *Farrell v. United States*, which was heard in the U.S. Supreme Court in 1878, a distiller (Farrell) and his sureties executed a bond on June 13, 1870, in the penal sum (a sum that represents the maximum amount a surety will pay under a bond, similar to an insurance policy limit) of $33,000, with the condition that it would be voided if they paid the government the amount of the taxes due on the 449 barrels of whiskey stored at Farrell's bonded warehouse in Peoria, Illinois, before the spirits were to be removed from the warehouse and within one year after the date of the bond.

On July 27, 1870, a fire burned down the warehouse and all the whiskey inside it. The warehouse had been in the charge of an internal revenue gauger. When the government came for its $16,116.50 tax payment, Farrell pleaded non est factum, a defense in contract law that allows a signing party to escape the performance of an agreement that is fundamentally different from what they intended to execute. They argued that they didn't owe any of the sum demanded, given that the whiskey no longer existed. The circuit court for the Northern District of Illinois thought otherwise and found in favor of the government. In affirming the decision, Supreme Court justice Strong provided:

> The obligation was unconditional, and it was exactly that which the distiller and his sureties were by the act of Congress required to assume. Depositing distilled spirits in a government warehouse did not make them the property of the government or cause them to be held at the risk of the bailee. The property remained in the distiller, and the risk of loss by fire or any other casualty was consequently his. He and his sureties undertook to pay the government tax upon the spirits in the warehouse within one year, with no exception for any possible contingency. The judgment of the court is correct. The case of the distiller may be a hard one, but his misfortune is not the fault of the government.

According to the opinion, it was on the distiller to have insurance on his whiskey, and it was unfortunate that a subsequent statute (enacted in May 1872) that provided for remission of a tax payment due in the event that distilled liquors were destroyed while in the custody of a revenue officer in a bonded warehouse was not applicable. The bonding period was increased to three years in 1879 and later increased to eight years to better aid the straight whiskey distillers. The increased bonding time allowed distillers to better attempt to compete with a type of whiskey producer known as a rectifier.

3

THE RISE OF THE RECTIFIERS

*U*ntil around 1830, straight whiskey was the only type of whiskey made in America. With the introduction of the continuous still, an instrument that allowed for the production of large amounts of grain neutral spirits (GNS) on a consistent basis, it became possible to make two new types of whiskey: rectified whiskey and blended whiskey. So, now, there was: (1) straight whiskey, (2) rectified whiskey that had a base of GNS that producers or rectifiers would filter, flavor, color or blend to fit their customers' wishes and (3) blended whiskey, which was a mixture of rectified whiskey and straight whiskey.

The term *rectified* or *rectification* came to mean, in the liquor trade, a process or procedure where distilled spirits were cut, blended, mixed or infused. A rectifier was one who took bulk GNS and tweaked it to change its character. The practice was to take the GNS, reduce it to the proper proof and then add coloring and flavoring to the compounds and perhaps a touch of straight whiskey to imitate the taste of straight whiskey, totally bypassing the expensive and time-consuming aging process. There was also no loss of product to absorption and evaporation. When the alcohol tax was reintroduced in 1862, the occupation "rectifier" had been added to those who were taxed. The definition of the occupation follows:

Every person who rectifies, purifies, or refines distilled spirits or wines by any process (other than original and continuous distillation, or original and continuous processing, from mash, wort, wash, or any other substance, through continuous closed vessels and pipes, until the production is complete), and every person who, without rectifying, purifying, or refining distilled spirits, shall by mixing such spirits, wine, or other liquor with any material, manufacture any spurious, imitation, or compound liquors for sale, under the name of whisky, brandy, rum, gin, wine, spirits, cordials, or wine bitters, or any other name, shall be regarded as a rectifier, and as being engaged in the business of rectifying.

Amazingly, the rectifier occupational tax remained a part of the Internal Revenue Code until it was repealed in 1979.

The first bonding statute in 1868 also recognized the rise of the rectified whiskey producer, providing that while straight whiskey was in a bonded warehouse:

No material nor substance of any kind other than pure water can be added during the process of bottling or the preparation of the spirits for bottling, nor can any substance or material be subtracted, nor can any method or process by applied to alter or change in any way the original conditions or character of the product, except as authorized by statute. The storekeeper or gauger will not, therefore, admit to the bottling house any material or substance capable of being incorporated with the spirits except pure water only.

Most rectifiers acted as wholesalers who purchased whiskey from distilleries to resell it to retailers, taverns and restaurants. Rectifiers could redistill, filter, flavor, color or blend their base GNS to fit the flavor profile of their intended customers. There was a small group of rectifiers that blended or mixed small amounts of straight whiskey with large amounts of GNS and sold that product as "straight whiskey." As described in the 1905 Kentucky Court of Appeals case *E.H. Taylor Jr. and Sons Co. v. Marion E. Taylor*, 27 Ky.L.Rptr., 124 Ky. 173, 85 S.W. 1085 (1905):

The [evidence] *shows that the rectifiers or blenders take a barrel of whisky, and draw off a large part of it, filling it with water, and then adding spirits or other chemicals to make it proof, and give it age, bead, etc. The* [evidence] *also shows that from 50 to 75 per cent of the whisky sold in the United States now is blended whisky, and that a large part of the trade prefer it to the straight goods. It is a cheaper article, and there is therefore a temptation to simulate the more expensive* [straight] *whisky.*

With upward of 85 percent of the market in the twenty years prior to Prohibition, rectified whiskey producers relied on numerous "guide" books that provided detailed instructions on how to make imitation liquors. These recipe books contained details on how to add and mix such items, including syrup, grains of paradise, wintergreen oil, dried peaches, brown sugar, caramel and prune and cherry juices. In the 1860 book *A Treatise on the Manufacture, Imitation, Adulteration, and Rectification of Foreign Wines, Brandies, Gins, Rums, Etc.*, the table of contents lists that it has detailed recipes for "Old Rye" whiskey, "Old Rye Monongahela," "Wheat" and "Bourbon" whiskeys. The 1874 book by Oliver Cotter titled *Adulterations of Liquors, with a Description of the Poisons Used in Their Manufacture* states:

> *The business of making adulterated liquors has been so simplified that any novice who knows enough to make a punch or cocktail can learn in a short time how to make any kind of liquor that will pass muster with nine tenths of the drinking community. The oil and essences are within the reach of any dealer, wholesale or retail, and with the chemical preparations he can procure the directions for making a large or small quantity in a short time....If the oils, essences, and other chemical preparations are wanted for converting corn whiskey into any other kind of liquor, they can easily be obtained.... To make old bourbon or rye and wheat whiskey, enough of these chemical compounds can be purchased for $8 to make four barrels.*

Cotter identified himself as "a reformed liquor dealer," and in his introduction to the book, he provided that he believed "that the true way to promote the temperance cause is to kindly and truthfully teach the people the true nature of alcoholic beverages and to expose the system of adulterations and frauds that are practiced to an alarming extent by the dealers."

Fusel oil was recognized as a dangerous ingredient that adversely affected the smell and taste of whiskey. Fusel alcohols, also called fuselol, furfurol or fusel oil, are mixtures of several alcohols produced as a byproduct during alcohol fermentation. The word *fusel* is a German word that means "bad liquor." The process of aging whiskey in a barrel was understood at the time to increase the presence of fusel oil. A U.S. Tariff Commission report, in discussing the use of new or reused oak barrels, states:

> *In general, whiskeys distilled at low proofs, such as heavy-bodied American whiskeys contain relatively more of the congeneric substances [such as fusel oils], and therefore benefit from storage in new cooperage. Whiskeys distilled*

at high proofs, such as light-bodied whiskeys that are the principal constituents of Canadian and Scotch whiskey, [also including most of the rectified whiskeys produced in the U.S.] *have most of the congeners removed in distillation, and so need not be stored in charred new oak cooperage.*

A 1901 *Washington Post* advertisement for a "Maryland Club Whiskey" that looked like a proper article was titled "Furfurol to Blame—This Harmful Agent Is Not to Be Found in Really Old Whiskey." It quotes the *London Lancet*, "It is now shown that comparatively speaking, at any rate, fusel oil is not the injurious constituent of whiskey." It continues, "Old, matured whiskey is free from furfurol, while freshly made or unmatured spirit contains a marked amount of this constituent, the source of the throbbing headache of the heavy drinker." The advertisement concludes, "In light of this recent discovery, new whiskey and good whiskey are incompatible terms, as far as the drinker is concerned."

Rectifying trade books treated fusel oil in various ways. Some added fusel oil to make the rectified whiskey bead like straight whiskey. Others contained detailed instructions for properly removing it with potentially dangerous chemicals. Still others included natural aromatic ingredients that were used to try to cover up the taste of the fusel oils rather than remove it. In Joseph Fleischman's 1885 book, *The Art of Blending and Compounding Liquors and Wines*, he argued that "[natural fruit and tea] flavoring extracts…are used in every rectifying establishment" and that there is "nothing injurious," whereas no honest rectifier should introduce "sulphuric acid, suphate of copper, oxalic acid, chloroform, acetate of potash and ammonia." Eventually, the rectifiers were so successful in removing fusel oil that its absence became a key trait used by regulators and in advertisements to distinguish between straight and rectified whiskey.

A recipe for imitation bourbon whiskey from Pierre Lacours's 1863 book titled *The Manufacture of Liquors, Wines and Cordials Without the Act of Distillation* read:

Rectified whiskey, thirty gallons; tincture of grains of paradise, one gallon; water, 9 gallons; mucilage of slippery elm bark, on half pint; acetic ether, three ounces; oil of wintergreen, fifteen drops dissolved in ether. This whiskey has the color usual to all rectified whiskies.

It seems history is repeating itself with the recent introduction of a whiskey made in California that is touted as "the first molecular whiskey," made overnight, primarily in a lab, using no actual traditional whiskey making techniques and starting with a neutral spirit as a base, a corn-based GNS and all the bits that make up a tiny percentage of the volume of the bottle but contain all the flavor.

Today, there are forty-one subtypes of alcohol defined under the class called whiskey with the U.S. Department of Treasury's Tax and Trade Bureau (TTB) regulation titled "The Standards of Identity for Distilled Spirits." The definition of the subtype of alcohol identified as "spirit whiskey" covers the products rectifiers made in the late nineteenth century, and it says, "a mixture of neutral spirits and not less than 5 percent on a proof gallon basis of whisky or straight whisky, or straight whisky and whisky, if the straight whisky component is less than 20 percent on a proof gallon basis." Basically, it's a mixture of straight whiskey and GNS, in which the whiskey content is at least 5 percent. TTB's definition of straight whiskey is "whiskey produced from a fermented mash of less than 51 percent of any one type of grain and stored in a charred new oak container for two years or more."

Most of the occupational taxes imposed at the beginning of the Civil War were repealed by 1870. But the taxes on alcohol and tobacco vocations were kept in place. In a 1976 Department of the Treasury report titled "Occupational Taxes on the Alcohol Industry Should be Repealed," it was explained that after 1870:

> *Occupational taxes in the alcohol industry apparently were continued because of their excellent revenue producing capabilities and a generally held belief that, by taxing the various alcohol industries, the cost would be transferred to the consumer and consumption would decrease. This philosophy was presented on the floor of the House of Representatives by the chairman of Ways and Means in the following statement: "I had hundreds of people coming to me and appealing to as why a man who deals in whiskey should be taxed more than a man who deals in clothing or leather, and I have answered that the articles in which he deals are supplied for an artificial appetite, that we must make the consumer pay for the indulgence."*

In arguing the repeal of the occupational tax on alcohol-related jobs, it was pointed out how the revenues from the taxes steadily declined over time. In 1908, the alcohol-related occupational taxes collected $7.3 million, representing 2.9 percent of the nation's internal revenue of $252 million. In 1974, the alcohol-related occupational taxes yielded only $18.4 million of the approximately $269 billion in revenue collected, or about one-ten-thousandth of 1 percent.

4

THE WAR TO DEFINE WHAT WHISKEY IS

he practice of rectification enabled its practitioners to undersell straight whiskey—so much so that by 1906, more than 85 percent of all the whiskey sold in the American market was rectified whiskey. Starting in the early 1890s, the distillers of straight whiskey began to fight back. The push for the national regulation of the whiskey industry came at the behest of the straight whiskey producers, who framed it as a legislative attempt to protect consumers from the dangerous rectifiers. Their primary concern was that rectifiers were knowingly selling whiskey adulterated with dangerous and poisonous ingredients that were undisclosed to the consumers.

As it turns out, this concern was not entirely based in fact. In 1882, a lecturer of toxicology at the Jefferson Medical College, Dr. Leffman, stated:

> *I am not one of those who believe that there is a large amount of injurious adulteration either in food or in drink. There is a good deal of fraud about the liquor business, but it does not extend to the use of poisonous drugs. The compounders have a good many harmless ways of doctoring liquors.*

In another lecture on the dangers of alcohol, Leffman argued, "It is often said that the harm done by liquor is on account of its adulteration, but it is a great mistake. The adulterations of liquor are not, as a rule, any more harmful that the original article. It is the alcohols which are in the genuine liquor which do the harm."

A Bit of American Whiskey History

A Drawing of Dr. Harvey W. Wiley from the October 12, 1913 *Alexandria Gazette*, reproduced here. *Library of Congress.*

It was hard for consumers to verify or know that the whiskey they were buying was accurately represented and unadulterated, because whiskey was commonly sold to consumers out of barrels. This was true for even the bonded whiskey that was stored in government-overseen warehouses, because up until 1893, the smallest allowable container that could be bonded was five gallons, which required the further splitting of the whiskey into small unit sizes for final sale to the consumer.

A group of distillers mostly from Kentucky, led by E.H. Taylor Jr., along with the then–U.S. Secretary of Treasury John G. Carlisle, who was a former congressman and senator from northern Kentucky, and Harvey W. Wiley, the chief of the Department of Agriculture's Bureau of Chemistry who would later be called the father of the Federal Drug Administration (FDA) and coincidentally grew up in northern Kentucky and came from a family involved in the straight whiskey business, were the main architects and consensus builders for both the 1897 Bottled-in-Bond Act and the 1906 Pure Food and Drug Act.

BOTTLED-IN-BOND ACT OF 1897

In describing how the 1897 Bottled-in-Bond Act was passed, Wiley said that rectifiers saved all the costs of making real whiskey in the following way:

> By the trick of making real "whisky" without any distillery at all making it ten years old "while you wait." But above all—and here is a point of particular interest—he decided to pretend that he did have a distillery and that the imitation whisky was the real article or a mixture of two real whiskies and that it, too, was rendered rigid in cost and therefore ridged in price, and he actually charged, and today often charges, more for his bogus whisky than the real distiller charges for the genuine.
>
> The wide margin of profit in this golden game of imitation, therefore, goes to the "rectifier" himself, and had not Congress passed the bottling in bond law in 1897, genuine whisky proper would have been practically eliminated as a plain economic proposition.
>
> This law has been a blow to the "rectifier" who cannot get the government stamp over the corks of his concoctions. The bottling-in-bond stamp is the line of cleavage between genuine and the bogus whiskies in glass.

With the Bottled-in-Bond Act of 1897, the straight whiskey producers got what amounted to a U.S. government guarantee of the authenticity of their whiskey. As explained in a Sixth Circuit Court of Appeals decision *W.A. Gaines and Co. v. Turner-Looker Co.*, 204 F. 553 (6th Cir. 1913), "the consumer received the government's solemn guarantee that the contents of the bottle were exactly as stated on the label and that there were no additives." It was not a guarantee of quality, but it was a guarantee of the purity and authenticity of the contents. The act provided that only straight whiskey could be bonded and further required that the whiskey be made at one distillery in one batch and be aged at least four years in warehouses supervised by government and be stored at 100 proof. The motive to pass the act was really just that straight distillers were seeking a form of protectionism against the rectifiers' cheaper and easier-to-produce product.

Though, legally, the tax stamp certified only that the taxes had been paid on the whiskey, straight whiskey producers sought to convince the public that the "bottled-in-bond" designation was equated with purity and high quality. The image on the following page is an advertisement from the June 27, 1899 *Evening Star*. Blended whiskey producers and rectifiers were unable to use the tax stamp because rectified alcohol was not aged and therefore not stored in bonded warehouses. Nonetheless, they were successful in garnering a large percentage of the market by promoting brand names, monitoring the quality of their goods and advertising to address quality assurance. The 1897 advertisement on the following page advised consumers to look out for fraud. Indeed, the Canadian Club's producers went so far as to take other producers selling imitation products to court. They also sent independent agents to ensure that retailers were selling their products unadulterated.

Produced by the makers of Canadian Club Whisky, the advertisement provides a bit of the background necessary to understand the whiskey war that pitted two sides of the industry (straight versus rectified) against each other. The following is from the November 30, 1910 edition of the *Evening Star*:

The Pure Food Law—A Magnificent Victory

Never was such a law more needed in this country, nor more welcome than to us, who have suffered enormously from the fraudulent imitation of popular labels. This law, some years ago, would have saved us hundreds of thousands of dollars. Yet, to our amazement, a law designed to protect honest manufacturers no less than the public was immediately made the

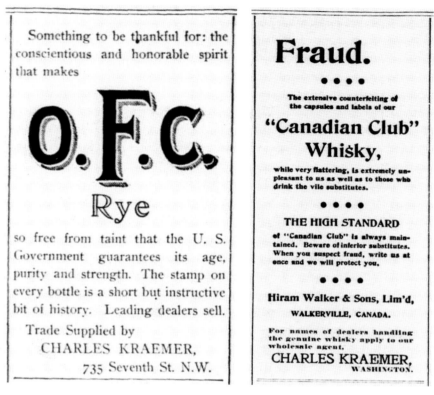

Left: An O.F.C. Rye advertisement from the June 27, 1899 *Washington Evening Star*, reproduced here. *Library of Congress.*

Right: A Canadian Club advertisement from the March 11, 1897 *Washington Evening Star*, reproduced here. *Library of Congress.*

pretext for an attack upon our worldwide and previously unimpeached reputation. After a costly contest, lasting four years, we have gained a signal and complete victory: in doing which, we have also shown that the law is the just measure it was intended to be.

We have not, as the public has been led to believe, obstructed the PURE FOOD LAW nor opposed the views of the GOVERNMENT. We have simply resisted a mere bureau's usurpation of authority and its novel and preposterous theories, submission to which would have driven us out of the American market.

The story is almost incredible and difficult to tell briefly; yet, in justice to ourselves and to the patrons who have remained so splendidly loyal to us, we must outline the facts.

For generations, the one universally recognized impurity of whisky has been FUSEL OIL, which we have always removed by distillation. The bureau referred to, as late as 1904, insisted that to be "good for consumption" whisky must have practically no FUSEL OIL.

Kentucky "straight whisky," when new, is rank with FUSEL OIL, but the makers always assured consumers that this noxious impurity was transformed by age into delightful ethers, etc. A few years ago, it was found that age makes no change in the FUSEL OIL, except to remove its vile odor. The Kentucky distillers, knowing well the aversion to FUSEL OIL, were in desperate straits; so, they boldly declared that REAL whisky new or old, must contain all the FUSEL OIL and denounced all REFINED WHISKY as a base imitation. And the bureau backed them up.

This is no pleasantry but sober fact. CANADIAN CLUB WHISKY was condemned, solely because it contains practically no FUSEL OIL.

Some months ago, President Taft, after a searching investigation by the solicitor general, overruled the bureau completely. Now the attorney general has decided that the PURE FOOD LAW does not require our label to be changed by a single letter.

At the WORLD'S COLUMBIAN EXPOSITION in 1893, Dr. H.W. Wiley, then, as now, chief of the bureau referred to, reported CANADIAN CLUB, to be "pure and fully up to the examination required," and, by authority of Congress, it received an award for "fine aroma, very pleasant taste, thorough maturity, purity and absence of alien matter," which expresses every excellence any whisky can possess. CANADIAN CLUB is the same now as then.

If any consumers really want FUSEL OIL in their whisky, they should use Kentucky "straight whisky": CANADIAN CLUB will not suit them. All who desire that the PURE FOOD LAW shall be rationally administered and not as a weapon of any one man, should send for our history of this remarkable case. Please name this paper.

HIRAM WALKER and SONS, Limited, Walkerville Ontario, Canada

The Pure Food Law mentioned in the article is the Pure Food and Drug Act of 1906, which was signed into law by President Theodore Roosevelt on June 30, 1906. Ostensibly seen as a measure exclusively for consumer protection, one aspect of the law revealed a deep split between whiskey producers; on one side were the makers of "straight whiskey" who supported the passage of the law, and on the other were rectified whiskey producers who vehemently opposed passage.

It was Harvey Wiley who was the chief proponent of this legislation. Since the passage of the Bottle-in-Bond Act, there were numerous bills that sought to regulate the processed food industry—all of which failed, due to the fact they all failed to gain the necessary traction to pass. Wiley was particularly interested in poisonous, adulterated and mislabeled foods. It was his position to define acceptable and unacceptable products according to whether they were "adulterated" with additives. To him, additives were, by definition, harmful because they were "unnatural." In his lobbying efforts to drum up support for the legislation, he also sought to make himself the administrator of the law—that is, to make the Chemistry Bureau responsible for enforcement of the law.

Dr. Harvey Wiley (1909). *Library of Congress.*

The Poison Squad

One of Wiley's more colorful publicity schemes used to inspire interest in the bill that would become the Pure Food Law was his creation of what would become to be known as the "Poison Squad." It was to be a five-year human feeding experiment that took place in the basement of the Bureau of Chemistry's headquarters, located on what is now Independence Avenue. He assembled a dozen volunteers and fed them seemingly wholesome meals that contained potentially harmful substances. The experiment was meant to test the effects of certain preservatives on the human body. The first five preservatives studied were borax, salicylic acid, sulfuric acid, sodium benzoate and formaldehyde. Dosages ranged from one-half gram daily to four grams a day by the end of the study. The volunteers knew they were consuming potentially poisonous foods, but they didn't know which of the foods contained the substances.

The Poison Squad became a pop culture sensation when newspaper reporters began interviewing the squad's chef through a basement window. In bowing to the incredible public interest, Wiley began to provide details of every experiment and the effects on the volunteers. The public, through the newspaper reports, followed every detail. The experiment even inspired poems and a minstrel show. As sung by Lew Dockstader in his minstrel company in Washington, D.C., during the week of October 4, 1903:

If ever you should visit the Smithsonian Institute,
Look out that Professor Wiley doesn't make you a recruit,
He's got a lot of fellows there that tell him how they feel.
They take a batch of poison every time they eat a meal.
For breakfast they get cyanide of live, coffin shaped.
For dinner, undertaker's pie, all trimmed with crepe;
For supper, arsenic fritters, fried in appetizing shade,
And late at night they get prussic acid lemonade

(CHORUS)
They may get over it, but they'll never look the same.
That kind of bill of fare would drive most men insane.
Next week, he'll give them moth ball, à la Newburgh, or else plain.
They may get over it, but they'll never be the same.

The experiments stopped after only a few months, when some of the chemicals made several of the volunteers very sick (nausea, vomiting, stomachaches, et cetera) and Wiley began to worry that the humorous banter about the squad would discredit the seriousness of the project. A May 24, 1904 article titled "Scientific Martyrdom of Poison Squad Over—Released From 'Death Diet' in Various Stages of Wrecked Health—None Fatally Affect by Preservatives" stated:

The famous poison squad on which Dr. Harvey Wiley has been experimenting has concluded its digestive heroics and today is enjoying the first meal in months which is not specially and deliberately loaded with salicylic, sulphuric or benzoic acid poisons.

It probably didn't help matters that Secretary of Agriculture James Wilson thought that Wiley was getting too much public attention and asked him to stop talking to the press about the squad.

Following a failure in 1903 to get the Pure Food Act passed, Wiley decided to strengthen his already established alliance with the straight whiskey producers—calculated to both increase the likelihood of the legislation passing and his control over the contents and administration of the bill. In doing so, he provoked the whiskey rectifiers, including their foreign contingent, who were represented by the National Wholesale Liquor Dealers, a trade organization led by Warwick M. Hough, a St. Louis attorney.

In the 1904 decision *Buttfield v. Stranahan*, 192 U.S. 470 (1904), the Supreme Court upheld the quality standards found in the 1897 Tea Importation Act, which blocked the importation of teas that failed to meet government standards for quality, purity and fitness for consumption. This decision raised alarm bells for the producers of rectified whiskeys. Fearing that any kind of legal food standard would be used to declare their products illegal, the rectifiers, along with the makers of chemically preserved foods, got together and collectively found a number of sympathetic senators whom they convinced to cut all appropriations for food standard work and also remove all provisions for legal food standards in the latest iteration of the pending food and drug bill. In a May 25, 1904 letter to a colleague, Wiley bitterly lamented, "I do not think any more vicious thing ever happened in the modern history of American legislation than this," concluding that "the first great legislative victory has been won by the opposition."

THE BATTLE TO PASS THE PURE FOOD AND DRUG ACT OF 1906

In an effort to garner public support for the legislation, Wiley chose the 1904 Louisiana Purchase Centennial Exposition, held in St. Louis, to stage his attack. At the exposition, he ensured that the pure food concerns were put in the public eye like never before. This is really the first salvo in the war between the straight whiskey producers and the rectifiers.

At the exposition, Wiley organized a Pure Food Congress, which was to rule on what foods should be considered pure. The committee that ruled on whiskey found that although rectified alcohol had fewer impurities in it than straight whiskey, it was the straight whiskey that was the "pure" product. Wiley officially maintained that only alcohol made from grain and aged in a barrel was whiskey. This, of course, excluded rectified alcohol from being called whiskey because it did not need to be stored in barrels to remove its impurities. Neither common usage nor chemical analysis justified this outcome. For more than one hundred years before aging in a barrel became a common practice, the term *whiskey* had been applied to any alcoholic beverage distilled from grain. Both straight and rectified products were nearly identical, chemically speaking. The main contents of both were ethyl alcohol and water. Straight whiskey contained larger amounts of poisonous fusel oil than rectified whiskey, and rectified whiskey sometimes had small amounts of coloring and flavoring that were absent from straight whiskey. These differences were minor, and there was no scientific basis in chemistry for Wiley's position.

Through Wiley's alliance with the straight whiskey producers, he secured the support and financing of a group whose objective was to gain a competitive advantage against the rectified producers. They sought to do so by lobbying for legislation that would brand rectified whiskey as an "imitation." For his part, Wiley labeled the rectified producers as the "Whiskey Trust," the enemies of pure and wholesome food.

Soon after the St. Louis Exposition, Wiley granted an extensive interview to the *Chicago American* newspaper that was later published as an article in newspapers across the country. The interview appeared under the headline "Whisky That is Not Whisky—American People Are Drinking Labels Instead of Real Thing, According to Dr. Wiley." In the article, Wiley declared that 85 percent of the so-called whiskey on the American market was not whiskey and that fake whiskey makers were a powerful force behind the opposition to pure food. Wiley also had this to say about rectifiers:

> *Now, a word as to how the "rectifier" works in making his spurious whiskies. There is a distilled spirit known to the trade as silent or neutral spirit, because it is silent as to its origin and neutral to all others. It is neither whisky, brandy, rum nor gin, but a colorless, odorless, tasteless product, which can be instantaneously transformed by the "blender" or "rectifier" into a fictious whisky, brandy, rum or gin by the addition of artificial essence or flavors, while by the use of caramel the bogus article can be made to look as though it had lain in charred barrels and abed for years. The trick is done overnight in tremendous volume and mammoth business houses flourish in the so-called whisky market foundationed on stupendous fraud.*

Wiley knew that he had no real ground for holding this position, and in testimony before Congress in 1904, he provided, "The government's stamp does guarantee purity in respect of the origin of the whiskey and its supervision by the government, but of course, it does not guarantee that it is pure in the sense of wholesomeness." Winning the battle for public opinion remained important for both Wiley and the whiskey rectifiers. Wiley went after the Scotch whiskey producers in an article titled "Another Doubt Raised—Dr. Wiley's Statement About Scotch Whisky Sets Consumers to Thinking" in the September 25, 1904 *Washington Post*. In the article, it was reported that Wiley had been investigating imported food and drink products to protect American consumers against

WHISKEY MAKERS IN WASHINGTON, D.C.

adulterations, and he raised doubts about the integrity of Scotch whiskey and claimed that the smoky flavor of the whiskey came "by the use of creosote." Creosote is an extremely flammable byproduct of wood combustion that consists mainly of tar. Traces of creosote are found in the smoke that rises from open flames. Creosote gives some smoked meats their distinctive flavors, scents and stability.

The Scotch whiskey producers fought back. In a *Washington Post* article dated January 26, 1905, titled "Prof. Wiley Denies Everything," a "staff correspondent" announced that Professor Wiley "had emphatically denied statements attributed to him in connection with [Scotch] whiskies," mainly that "the smoky flavor of Scotch, which so many of us pretend to enjoy, is imparted by means of creosote." The article went on:

Now comes Prof. Wiley, with eye disheveled and hair in fine frenzy rolling, denying his alleged denial and issuing a fresh proclamation of his faith. He declares that 85 percent of our American whisky is adulterated, as previously announced, and indignantly repels the suggestion that he ever for a moment wobbled on that oracle.

Prof. Wiley scorns and blasts the imputation that he ever said that he didn't say our whisky is adulterated, and upon that proud platform, with one hand buried in his coat and his expressive legs discoursing incidental music, he brands the allegation and defies the allegator.

Is our whisky adulterated, and if so, is the adulteration pernicious or merely unimportant? The paternal government, which provides Prof. Wiley for our enlightenment and guidance—along with a countless number of prophets in other departments of problematic usefulness—has given us a nudge. The whisky in common use is not what it purports to be, but, on the contrary, very considerably something else. What are we going to do about it?

Wiley struck back in a *Washington Post* article titled "Scotch Whisky," dated March 24, 1906:

Prof. Wiley has at last completed his inquisition into the imported articles known, respectively, as "Scotch" and "Irish" whisky, and the whole country now knows what The Post *has long suspected and frequently intimated, that they are frauds and humbugs both.*

We suggest, therefore, that since nine-tenths of this so-called Scotch whisky is the distilled product of inferior European corn, and the only exotic features thereof are a bad smell and a rancid taste, it may be just as well, if not better, to have our American corn juice and the dead-cat effect added by the employment of domestic material.

The domestic rectifiers got into the game as well. In a March 5, 1906 *Evening Star* article titled "Pure Whiskey," there was a bold subheading that read, "**IMPURE WHISKEY Is a Whiskey Containing a Large Amount of Impurities**," and the article went on to provide two quotes attributed to Wiley:

The term Fusel Oil *means a collection of these higher alcohols which are produced in the fermentation of mash. These alcohols, however, pass over with the water in the still. Some of them have higher boiling points, but they are carried over mechanically so that they all appear in greater or less quantities in the product. Now in order that this product be good for consumption, it is necessary that this Fusel Oil be removed.*
—*statement of Dr. H.W. Wiley before the Pure Food Congress*

The government does not guarantee the purity.
—*statement of Dr. H.W. Wiley before Senate Committee on Manufactures*

Under another bold subheading, "**Bottled in Bond Whiskeys Most Impure—As Shown by Recent Prosecutions Under Pure-Food Laws of Minnesota**," the article states:

Bottled-in-Bond is the alluring and reassuring labels on bottles of whiskey which are being sold to retail dealers in the Twin Cities, and by them, dispensed to patrons. Analysis by the chemists employed by the Diary and Food Department of the state shows that in many instances the whiskey contains enough Fusel Oil to kill a guinea pig.
—St. Paul Dispatch, *Thursday, January 5, 1905*

It is quite natural that any distiller, finding himself with a lot of poor goods on hand, should seek some way to get rid of what he cannot sell to his regular wholesale customers, so he bottles it in bond, depends on the little green stamp to help him work it off on an unsuspecting public.
—De Bar's Circular

Under the final bold subheading in the article, "**Rectification Alone Produces Pure Whiskey**," the article states, in part:

The manufacturer of whiskey or any other alcoholic liquors rarely purifies the products but disposes of them to the rectifying distiller, whose business is to remove from them any contaminations which render them disagreeable or highly injurious.
—Muspratt, 99

The previous article was likely an attempt to counter Wiley appearing to change his tune on fusel oil in a February 1906 hearing, where he spoke before the House Committee on Ways and Means, as captured in the February 10, 1906 *Evening Star* article "Danger of Fusel Oil, Dr. Wiley Contradicts the General Impression." In the article, the following was captured:

Fusel Oil Not a Poison

"Then fusel oil is an alcohol?" asked Chairman [Serano] *Payne* [Republican, New York].
"Yes, it is an amyl alcohol," responded Dr. Wiley.
"Fusel oil is very poisonous, is it not?" continued Payne.
"Oh, fusel oil is not so deadly," replied Dr. Wiley, scornfully.
"I always understood it was poison," said the chairman, interested in pursuing the subject.
"That is a mistake," emphatically declared the government food expert. "It is rather a pleasant drink."
In view of the fact that all other leading chemist[s] *regard fusel oil as very poisonous, Dr. Wiley's statement will undoubtedly cause much comment in the scientific world. It is thought likely, however, that it is one of his "scientific pleasantries," like his statement regarding artificial honey in the comb, artificial lamb chops and imitation whisky.*

Given his stature and position at the Department of Agriculture, Wiley had direct access to the members of Congress who would ultimately vote on and pass the Pure Food Act. He took full advantage. In an appearance before the members of the House Committee on Interstate and Foreign Commerce in late February 1906, Wiley not only made a plea for the bottled-in-bond whiskeys in preference to those which were not, he also put on a show for the members, actually making four different rectified liquors during his "tipple talk."

As captured in the February 28, 1906 *Washington Post* article titled "Prof. Wiley on Drinks—Shows House Committee How Whisky Is Made,

Smiles and Samples Blend," Wiley said, "[B]lended whiskies, compared with straight whiskies, are like the forms used by dressmakers on which to display gowns compared with real girls." His making of rectified alcohol was portrayed as follows:

> *He had a lot of glass tubes, graduates and other apparatus used in chemical experiments brought in, and he told the committee that he would make them four different kinds of whisky without the use of any whisky.*
>
> *All he had was a bottle filled with ethyl alcohol, a tube containing caramel or burnt sugar for coloring purposes and some water and some flavor extracts. He began mixing up the stuff, and when it was colored, he poured a bit of flavoring extract into a graduate and handed it out.*
>
> *"This, gentlemen, is Scotch whisky, a little dark in color, but Scotch," Prof. Wiley said. The graduate was sniffed at, snuffed at and tasted by some. All who could judge agreed that it was mighty poor substitute.*
>
> *"But I'm not a professional rectifier," Prof. Wiley said. The concoction smelled like a newly paved asphalt street, but Dr. Wiley, after a sniff or two, declared it had the "smoky smell" of Scotch.*
>
> *Makes Booze "While You Wait"*
>
> *Bourbon and rye were next made from the same stock, with the exception that different flavoring extracts were used.*
>
> *The bourbon and rye each had "aging oil" dropped in, which made the mixture look a bit more like red whiskey, and Dr. Wiley said the stuff was "fourteen years old." The final experiment was in making brandy from the same stock as the others.*

In the lead-up to the vote on the bill, the whiskey rectifiers successfully lobbied House members to remove a provision from the bill that would have required the listing of added ingredients to rectified whiskeys. They also lobbied for an amendment to allow the rectifiers to call their product "compounded" or "blended" whiskey. Without such a provision, they were worried that an administrative ruling by Wiley would require them to label their product "imitation" whiskey.

The debate that led to the passage of the bill in the House was reported to have been "exhaustive," with many representatives speaking on behalf of both sides. One particular representative's stunt during the debate was widely reported. A Democrat from Kentucky named Augustus Owsley

Stanley made a speech on behalf of the straight whiskey producers that channeled one of Wiley's previous appearances. In the June 24, 1906 edition of the *Evening Star*, under the subheading "Mr. Stanley Breaks Loose," it was reported that Stanley was in front of the speaker's desk to demonstrate how the "blender" makes "blended" whisky:

He was very much in earnest and, with high-pitched voice, said he stood before the House in the name of the health of the American people, in the name of honesty in enterprise and business, "just as much for honest whisky as for everything else."

[A representative from New York] *sought to interrupt him, but he waved him down by saying he would not yield to anybody. He said he had no objection to anybody blending two kinds of whisky, but he did object to making whisky while you wait. Then, taking a bottle from the table, he poured it into a graduate and said: "Here is a quart of alcohol, one hundred proof strong. It will eat the intestines out of a coyote. It will make a howling dervish out of an anchorite. It will make a rabbit spit in a bulldog's face. It is pure alcohol, and under the skill of a rectifier, he will put in a little coloring matter and then a little bead oil.* [Illustrating] *I drop that in it. Then I get a little essence of bourbon whisky, and there is no connoisseur in this House who can tell that hellish business from the genuine article.* [Applause] *I say that the coloring matter is not harmful, I say that the caramels are not harmful, but I say that the body stock of the whisky I made is rank alcohol, and when it gets into a man, it is pure hell."*

The bill passed the House with a vote of 241–17. The Senate and House bills were reconciled in conference and approved with no further discussion, and President Roosevelt signed it into law four days later on June 30, 1906. The newly passed law's first sentence provides: "An act for preventing the manufacture, sale, or transportation of adulterated or misbranded or poisonous or deleterious foods, drugs, medicines and liquors, and for regulating traffic therein and for other purposes."

Sections 8 and 9 of the Act specifically address whiskey misbranding:

Section 8
In the case of articles labeled, branded, or tagged so as to plainly indicate that they are compounds, imitations, or blends, and the word "compound," "imitation" or "blend," as the case may be, is plainly stated on the package in which it is offered for sale: Provided, that the term blend *as*

used herein shall be construed to mean a mixture of like substances, not excluding harmless coloring or flavoring ingredients used for the purpose of coloring or flavoring only: And provided further, that nothing in this act shall be construed as requiring or compelling proprietors or manufacturers of proprietary foods which contain no unwholesome added ingredients to disclose their trade formulas.

Section 9
That no dealer shall be prosecuted under the provisions of this act when he can establish a guarantee signed by the wholesaler, jobber, manufacturer or other party residing in the United States, from whom he purchases such articles to the effect that the same is not adulterated or misbranded within the meaning of this act, designating it.

Said guarantee, to afford protection, shall contain the name and address of the party or parties making the sale of such articles to such dealer, and such case said party or parties shall be amendable to the prosecutions, fines and other penalties which would attach, in due course, to the dealer under the provisions of this act.

THE LIQUOR SQUAD

After the bill was signed into law, Agriculture Secretary Wilson appointed Wiley chairman of the interdepartmental committee charged with administering the act. And that is when the real fun began. Rectifiers began all manner of moves to nullify or change the requirements of the act and sought to find sympathetic governmental figures to change things. Wiley, affectionately known as "Old Borax" by his fellow scientists, asked Congress to fund a study to determine the effect of alcohol on the human stomach. The October 17, 1906 *Washington Post* article titled "Liquor Squad This Time" described some unforeseen enthusiasm for his proposal:

Of course, nearly everybody has an idea that "booze" has a deleterious effect on the system in general and the stomach in particular; that an intemperate use of strong drink is followed by what is technically known as the "big head," while continued use of the fire water produces what is known as "snakes." But Dr. Wiley wants the facts, scientific facts, and to his mind, nothing brings out the facts quite so well as scientific experiments.

Another *Washington Post* article, this one dated October 28, 1906, and titled "Thirsty Men Proclaim Willingness to Enter Wiley's Whiskey Squad," has to be seen to be believed:

> *In announcing his contemplated experiments, he allowed it to be understood that he would try on his victims all of the standard brands of whiskies, brandies, gins, rums, cordials, wines, beers and ales. In less than two days after this announcement was printed in the newspapers, the tip got out all over hoboland that Washington was going to be a pretty soft place in which to put in the approaching winter. Hoboes at once began to drop in on Dr. Wiley at his office.*
>
> *When Dr. Wiley reached his office in the Department of Agriculture on the morning following the announcement of the investigation, he found one of the candidates for a martyr's tomb waiting for him in the hall. This one had the general exterior of Roaming Riley, the Traveling Thirst, and he shuffled right into the office in the chemist's footsteps.*
>
> *"Hey, Doc," he inquired hoarsely, "is dis booze gag o' your'n on de level?"*
>
> *"Please make your question a little clearer," suggested the chemist, who is something of a precisian and shy on colloquialisms. "What is it you wish to know?"*
>
> *"Dis suds t'ing," elaborated the chemist's red-nosed visitor. "Dis frame-up I'm after readin' about where your're goin' try t' pickle a bunch of rum-eaters. How 'bout it? Does it go?"*
>
> *Dr. Wiley started some evasive reply to the effect that he had considered something of the sort, but that he hadn't entirely arranged the details, and that—*
>
> *"Oh, Doc, let's begin now," put in the visitor, with an ingratiating grin on his face, and the chemist had to back into his private office and close the door before that candidate would take the hint and his departure.*

And the following is another episode from the article, describing Wiley's interaction with another candidate:

> *"This isn't any cure thing, is it?" inquired the nervous little man, looking furtively around the office. "It's not just a put up job to cure people of the liquor habit, I hope? After reading about this thing last evening, I dreamt last night that the whole business was just a scheme of the government's to stop people from drinking liquor, and I dreamt that the liquor you intended to serve out would be doped with some of the cure stuff and—"*

"Don't worry—it will all be doped with the kill stuff, certain enough,"
put in the chemist, reassuringly, and then the nervous little man insisted that
his name and address be taken down so that he could be sent for just as soon
as the rum squad was in process of organization.
"You wouldn't care to be cured of the drinking habit, then?" suggested
Dr. Wiley, as the nervous little man was about to pass out.
"Well, you see," replied the candidate with all the solemnity in the
world and without even the symptom of a smile, "I've already been cured
fourteen times in the last nine years, and as between the cures and the
booze, I'll take the booze. Anyhow, I haven't got much left now except
my thirst, and if I were to lose that, where'd be the fun and what 'ud be
the use?"

Sadly, though perhaps understandably, Congress did not authorize the funding for the project, so the Liquor Squad never came to be. Wiley turned his attention to his role in implementing and enforcing the Pure Food Act.

With the passage of the Pure Food Act, one might think that it was game over for the rectifiers—that the straight whiskey crowd had won the war. In reality, the games were just starting. In 1929, Wiley wrote a book setting out his version of the fight called *History of a Crime Against the Food Law*. In chapter 4 of the book, "What Is Whisky?" subtitled, "Rectified Whisky, the First Cause of Paralyzing the Food Law," he starts with his definition:

Whisky is a distillate, in a pot still, of fermented mash of a cereal or
mixture of cereals, containing all the natural elements of the grain and
ethyl alcohol and its congeners, volatile at the temperatures of distillation. It
contains also the coloring matters and other soluble products extracted from
the wood (oak), in which it is stored and any new compounds arising during
storage. Potable whisky is kept in storage for four years.
—definition by Bureau of Chemistry

It is the last sentence that caused so much controversy. He provides a detailed account of the back and forth between the straight whiskey and rectifier contingents and the politicians and judges they were allied with. It's a fascinating story that newspaper accounts struggled to fully capture.

Executive and Judicial Branch Actions

After the passage of the Pure Food Act, Wiley was in charge of enforcement and issued Food Inspection Decision (FID) 45, which covered "blended whiskies." Rectifiers, anxious to know how the government would regulate the use of the term *whiskey* on labels, sought clarity. In response to their questions, James Wilson, the secretary of agriculture, wrote on December 1, 1906:

> *The question presented is whether neutral spirits may be added to bourbon whisky in varying quantities, colored and flavored and the resulting mixture be labeled "blended whiskies." To permit the use of the word "whiskies" in the described mixture is to admit that flavor and color can be added to neutral spirits and the resulting mixture be labeled "whisky." The department is of the opinion that the mixtures presented cannot legally be labeled either "blended whiskies" or "blended whisky."…If neutral spirit, also known as cologne spirit, silent spirit or alcohol, be diluted with water to a proper proof for consumption and artificially colored and flavoured, it does not become a whisky, but a "spurious imitation."*

Though this response was signed by Secretary Wilson, within two months, apparently, Wilson had changed his mind. In February 1907, Wiley was summoned to appear before Wilson, along with the Department of Agriculture's solicitor George P. McCabe and Assistant Secretary Willet M. Hayes. In this meeting at the department headquarters at Fourteenth and B Streets Southwest, Wiley confirmed that he agreed with the response, and when Wilson asked Hayes for his opinion on the matter, he agreed with Wiley. When Solicitor McCabe was asked, however, he replied, "Dr. Wiley's definition of whisky is absurd. Whisky is any alcoholic beverage made from grain, properly colored and flavored, according to the prevailing custom of trade." Wilson indicated that he agreed with his solicitor, and Wiley tried to argue that under the act, only the Bureau of Chemistry could make a determination as to what constituted misbranding or the adulteration of food and drugs. To that, Secretary Wilson replied, "I will not take your construction of the law but that of my solicitor; that is what he is here for, to interpret the law to me." According to Wiley, this episode was the act that "constituted the first abrogation of the [act] by executive authority and laid the foundation for a succession of similar violations."

CHARLES J. BONAPARTE.

Above: The Department of Agriculture building (1909). *Library of Congress*.

Left: Attorney General Charles Bonaparte from the December 27, 1903 *Washington Times*, reproduced here. *Library of Congress*.

So, what did Wiley do? He immediately sought an audience with President Roosevelt through his secretary William Loeb Jr., getting Loeb to "acquaint the president of what had happened and to get a promise from, if possible, that he would not give his approval to [the] Wilson decision until [Wiley] had an opportunity to lay the whole matter before him." Wiley knew Loeb through their membership at the Cosmos Club, a Washington, D.C. private social club founded in 1878 as a gentlemen's club and located at 2121 Massachusetts Avenue Northwest. In the meantime, news of Wilson's reversal of position was leaked to the press, and rectifiers all over the country rejoiced the impending repeal of FID 45.

Within two weeks, Wiley was granted an audience with Roosevelt, and he resorted to his old experiment of making "whisky while you wait" for the president:

> *For two hours, I performed experiments, showing the president how all kinds of rectified whisky, brandy and rum could be made in a minute. At the close of the lecture, he came around to my side of the table and grasped my hand, saying to me, "Dr. Wiley, I have heard nothing but whisky for the last three weeks, and you are the first person who has ever given me a single idea that I can comprehend." Then, turning to Mr. Loeb, he said, "Send all these documents and samples to Mr. Bonaparte* [Attorney General Charles J. Bonaparte, the grandson of Napoleon's youngest brother, Jerome] *and ask Mr. Bonaparte to advise me on this question." Mr. Bonaparte did advise him. He sustained every single point that had been presented.*

The decision issued by Bonaparte and endorsed by Roosevelt was captured in FID 65, titled "The Labeling of Whisky, Blends, Compounds and Imitations Thereof." In an April 12, 1907 *Washington Post* article titled "Applying Whiskey Rule—President's Order Will Soon Be Put into Effect—Litigation Seems Probable," it was reported that the Pure Food Act would permit the use of four different labels in the whiskey trade. A close look at the actual language from Bonaparte's opinion shows, according to Wiley at least, that it was a "blend of legal learning and charming sarcasm."

> *I concede that a combination of whisky with ethyl alcohol, supposing, of course, that there is enough whisky in it to make it a real compound and not the semblance of one, may be fairly called "whisky"; provided the name is accompanied by the word "compound" or "compounded,"*

and provided a statement of the presence of another spirit is included in substance in the title.

The following seem to me appropriate specimen brands or labels for (1) "straight" whisky, (2) a mixture of two or more "straight" whiskies, (3) a mixture of "straight" whisky and ethyl alcohol and (4) ethyl alcohol flavored and colored so as to taste, smell and look like whisky:

(1) Semper Idem [always the same] *Whisky: A pure, straight whisky mellowed by age.*

(2) E Pluribus Unum [out of many, one] *Whiskey: A blend of pure, straight whiskies with all the merits of each.*

(3) Modern Improved Whisky: A compound of pure grain distillates, mellow and free from harmful impurities.

(4) Something Better than Whisky: An imitation under the pure food law, free from fusel oil and other impurities.

In the *Washington Post* article, the new required labels were reported to be:

(1) "Whisky" or "Straight Whiskey." This will be used upon bottles containing whisky which has been purified by aging in a charred barrel.

(2) "Blended Whisky." The contents of bottles with this label upon them will be the product obtained by mixing two or more straight whiskies, as, for example, the mixture of corn whisky and straight rye whisky.

(3) "Compound of Whiskey, with pure grain distillate," or "Whisky Compounded." This label will be used in place of many that are now marked blended whisky.

(4) "Imitation Whisky." It will be ethyl alcohol or neutral spirits free from fusel oil and other impurities, colored and flavoured so as to taste, smell and look like whisky.

Obviously, the rectified crowd was not pleased with Bonaparte's opinion. They quickly went to court, seeking to have FID 45 and FID 65 declared illegal and void. They brought their first case before the Federal District Court, sitting in Cincinnati, a center of the rectifying industry. According to Wiley, "rectifiers had been making, in that city, compounded and imitation whiskies designated by high-sounding names and sold under claims of great age." This product was derisively known locally as "Nigger whisky." The income from these spurious whiskeys was too large to be given up without a struggle. The judge assigned to the case apparently had close personal friendships with many of the rectifiers in the area. Despite these factors, the rectifiers experienced a crushing defeat when the judge issued an order that completely vindicated both of Bonaparte's opinions.

The rectifiers then sought favorable ruling in other federal courts, such as the courts in Springfield, Illinois; Covington, Kentucky; Indianapolis, Indiana; Buffalo, New York; Baltimore, Maryland; and San Francisco, California. But they lost in all these jurisdictions. In a decision from the court in the Southern District of Illinois, Judge Humphreys found:

> *The record also shows that diluted spirits treated with artificial coloring matter and essences are not sold to the trade as such but are always presented under such labels, terms and descriptions as import age and maturity and which the consumer identifies with the genuine product whisky.*

Finding the courts hostile, the rectifiers turned their efforts to back to the executive branch.

During this same time, on the other side of the equation, Bonaparte was eager to go on the offensive to enforce the law—through either criminal or seizure actions. The court shot him down on the criminal actions, but he did succeed in seven cases of seizure actions (this is, actions in rem). In every case, each of the courts affirmed Bonaparte's opinions on whiskey. The following are brief extracts from two such case decisions:

> *Case 2. Notice of Judgement 45.* United States v. 4 Barrels of Liquid Purporting to be Whisky. *This case was brought in the District of Columbia, Case No. 790. The libel alleged that the product was 4 "colored and mixed by the addition of coloring matter," in a manner whereby inferiority is concealed and in order to imitate old mature whisky and whereby the said product does imitate and appear to be old mature whisky. The judge issued the decree of condemnation on March 13, 1909.*

> *Case 4. Notice of Judgement 112.* United States v. 10 Cases of Quinine-Whisky, *Case No. 10142, the Honorable Kenesaw M. Landis, Northern District of Illinois presiding. The goods were ordered destroyed or to released on a bond of $1,000. Not to be sold contrary to the Food and Drugs Act, as is usual in such cases. Date of Judgement, November 20, 1909.*

After hanging up his robe, Landis became the first commissioner of Major League Baseball and is famous for being the guy that handled the "Black Sox" scandal, which saw him permanently expel eight members of the Chicago White Sox for conspiring to lose the 1919 World Series. The "M." in his name stands for "Mountain." His father fought in and was wounded at the major Civil War skirmish knows as the Battle of Kennesaw Mountain.

Redoubling their efforts to put pressure on the Roosevelt administration, the rectifiers turned up the heat on the members of Congress who were sympathetic to their interests. The rectifiers made a proposal to the president through several influential senators that they would withdraw all of their ongoing court cases to set aside the act if the act was modified to suit their needs. Finally caving in, in the winter of 1907, Roosevelt appointed a "Whisky Commission" that comprised Secretary of Agriculture Wilson, the associate chief of the Bureau of Chemistry Dr. F.L. Dunlap and the head of the Bureau of Internal Revenue of the Treasury Department John Capers. The purpose of the commission was to reopen the question decided by Bonaparte's earlier opinion. According to Wiley, Wilson and Capers were known advocates of the views of the rectified whiskey interests, and Dunlap "had shown a strong disposition to dissent from the existing rulings of the government." Apparently, the workings and even the existence of the commission were somewhat a mystery. Its existence was leaked to the press, but the members would not provide any details about what they were up to. In a letter to the president dated December 17, 1907, Dunlap, speaking for the commission, stated:

> *Under the Pure Food Law as administered now, neutral spirits, diluted to proper strength and colored with caramel, must be marked "Imitation Whiskey." The spirit distillers request that this name not be forced upon them but that they may use in its place one of the three names, "neutral whisky," "rectified whisky" or "redistilled whisky." It is my opinion that the term "whisky" should not be denied to neutral spirits diluted with water to a proper strength and colored with caramel. I believe that the use of the term "whisky" on such a product should be qualified by some term which carry notice to the consumer of the nature of the product. For this purpose, the term "neutral whisky," "redistilled whisky" and "rectified whisky" have been suggested.*

The politics at the Department of Agriculture were now complicated. On the straight whiskey side, there was President Roosevelt, who backed the opinions of Attorney General Bonaparte and those of Wiley. On the other side was Agriculture Secretary Wilson, Solicitor McCabe and the assistant chief of the Chemistry Bureau Dunlap, along with the other member of the "Whisky Commission," Capers from the Treasury Department. As Wiley reported it, Bonaparte was in an embarrassing position, having already rendered his opinion with reference to the nature of whiskey and the proper methods of labeling it. Roosevelt had sent to him the commission's report with a request for his opinion on it:

> *Two questions presented themselves to Mr. Bonaparte—whether he should reverse himself and accept the* [commission's] *findings, or whether he should stand neutral and idle, in case President Roosevelt should see fit to put into effect his commission's recommendations.* [He] *decided both of these points negatively.*
>
> *In a rather scathing letter to the president, he noted that the assistant chemist of the Department of Agriculture* [Dunlap] *suggests that on the question of the construction of a statute (the Pure Food Law), a very carefully considered and reconsidered opinion of the attorney general should be disregarded, he went on to say he could not fail to recognize Dr. Dunlap's recommendation a challenge of the correctness of his conclusion* [and to cite a number of the opinions from the court cases that already had been decided].

And for good measure, even though there were only a few weeks left before Bonaparte would leave office, he made it known to Roosevelt that he would "be compelled to resign in the event the president saw fit to overrule his decision on the whisky matter." Roosevelt had been mostly animated by his own sense of fair play in giving the rectifiers an opportunity to put forth their ideas; and now, he finally made his stand in backing Bonaparte and reaffirming the marking and labeling approach set out in Bonaparte's opinion. A February 27, 1909 *Washington Herald* editorial proclaimed:

VICTORIOUS MR. BONAPARTE

> *Our good right hand, palm up, to Mr. Charles Joseph Bonaparte in warm congratulations extended! "Whisky is Whisky, and nothing else is Whisky," say the attorney general; and so sayeth his chief, the president of the United States!*
>
> *We regard this as a great victory for the common people, and we trust they appreciate fully its momentous significance. Heretofore, every old thing*

that could assume the most remote whisky-like disguise has labeled itself
whisky and posed in the open market as the real, genuine, simon-pure article.

The "simon-pure" reference comes from the phrase "the real Simon Pure" (the true person or article) from the character Simon Pure (who is impersonated by another and obligated to prove his identity in Susanna Cenlivre's 1717 play *A Bold Stroke for a Wife*).

This victory was short-lived, however, lasting just ten months from February 19, 1909, to December 26, 1909. After entering office in early March 1909, President William H. Taft ordered a rehearing of the whiskey issue following a concerted lobbying campaign by the rectifiers to have Taft reverse the Roosevelt rulings so they could place their neutral spirits on the market under the name "whiskey." Taft appointed his solicitor general Lloyd Bowers to conduct the new look into whiskey. Bowers was a former classmate and fellow member of the Skull and Bones with Taft at Yale. Bowers's daughter later married Taft's oldest son. When it was finished, the printed version of the testimony in the matter, titled "Proceedings Before and By the Direction of the President Concerning the Meaning of Whisky," was a hefty 1,328 pages long.

Bowers's work was guided by Executive Order 1061, dated April 8, 1909, titled "Ordering Solicitor General to Report to President Branding Requirements for Whisky" and asked the following questions:

1. *What are the article whisky as known (1) to manufacturers, (2) to the trade, and (3) to the consumers at and prior to the date of the passage of the Pure Food Law?*
2. *What did the term* whisky *include?*
3. *Was there included in the term* whisky *any maximum or minimum congeneric substances as necessary in order that distilled spirits should be properly designated whisky?*
4. *Was there any abuse in the application of the term* whisky *to articles not properly failing within the definition of that term at and prior to the passage of the Pure Food Law, which it was the intention of Congress to correct by the provision of the Act?*
5. *Is the term* whisky *as a drug applicable to a different product than whisky as a beverage? If so, in what particulars?*

On May 24, 1909, Bowers submitted his report to the president, and it was universally condemned by all sides—so much so that they all appealed to Taft for help. At the first of many hearings held at the White House on June 28, 1909, all parties were represented and pleaded their cases to Taft over the next few months. On December 26, 1909, Taft rendered his decision, and when it was published the next day, it was front-page news in all newspapers. The opinion reversed Bowers's findings and ran contrary to "Roosevelt-Bonaparte-Wiley" orders and to many of the previous federal court rulings. As Wiley characterized it, "No higher flight of open contempt of judicial findings have ever been made by anyone whose duty it is to follow the courts' decisions." The *Evening Star* reported the decision with the headline:

> *HIS FINAL DECISION*
> *President Taft's Directions for Branding of Liquor*
> *AN ERROR OF SCIENTISTS*
> *What Name of Whisky Has Included Past Hundred Years*
> *CHEMISTS HAVE BEEN WRONG*

> [In the Decision,] *the president takes Dr. Wiley and other chemist[s] to task for a "fundamental error" as to what the name "whisky" has included during the past 100 years, and he also expresses the opinion that Mr. Bowers makes "too much a distinction" in his deductions.*

> *After an examination of all the evidence, it seems to me overwhelmingly established that for a hundred years, the term* whisky *in the trade and among the customers has included all potable liquor distilled from grain; that the straight whisky is, as compared with the whisky made by rectification or redistillation and flavoring and coloring matter, a subsequent improvement, and that therefore, it is a perversion of the pure food act to attempt now to limit the meaning of the term* whisky *to that which modern manufacture and taste have made the most desirable variety.*

The following is an extract from Taft's opinion:

> *The term* straight whisky *is well understood in the trade and well understood by consumers. There is no reason, therefore, why those who make straight whisky may not have the brand upon their barrels of straight whisky, with further descriptive terms as* bourbon *or* rye *whisky, as the composition of the grain used may justify, and they many properly add, if they choose, that it is aged in the wood.*

> *Those who make whisky of "rectified," "redistilled" or "neutral" spirits cannot complain if, in order to prevent further frauds, they are required to use*

a brand which shall show exactly the kind of whisky they are selling. For that reason, it seems fair to require them to brand their product as "whisky made from rectified spirits," or "whisky made from redistilled spirits," or whisky made from neutral spirits," as the case may be; and if aged in the wood, as sometimes is the case with this class of whiskies, they may add this fact.

A great deal of the liquor sold is a mixture of straight whisky with whisky made from neutral spirits. Now, the question is whether this ought to be regarded compound or blend. The Pure Food Law provides that "in the case of articles, branded or tagged so as to plainly indicate that they are compounds, imitations, or blends," the term blend *shall be construed to mean a mixture of like substances, not excluding harmless coloring or flavoring ingredients used for the purpose of coloring or flavoring only. It seems to me that straight whisky and whisky made from neutral spirits, each with more than 99½ percent ethyl alcohol and water, and with less than half of 1 percent of fusel oil, are clearly a mixture of like substances, and that while the latter may have and often does have burnt sugar or caramel to flavor and color it, such coloring and flavoring ingredients may be regarded as for flavoring and coloring only, because the use of burnt sugar to color and flavor spirits as whisky is much older than the coloring and flavoring by the tannin of the charred bark. Therefore, where straight whisky and whisky made from neutral spirits are mixed, it is proper to call them a blend of straight whisky and whisky made from neutral spirits.*

Canadian Club Whisky is a blend of whisky made from neutral spirits and of straight whisky aged in wood, and its owners and vendors are entitled to brand it as such.

By such an order as this decision indicates, the public will be made to know exactly the kind of whisky they buy and drink. If they desire straight whisky, then they can secure it by purchasing what is branded "straight whisky." If they are willing to drink whisky made from neutral spirits, then they can buy it under a brand showing it; and if they are content with a blend of flavors made by the mixture of straight whisky and whisky made of neutral spirits, the brand of the blend upon the package will enable them to buy and drink that which they desire. This is the intent of the act. It injures no man's lawful business, because it only insists upon the statement of the truth in the label. If those who manufacture whisky made from neutral spirits and wish to call it "whisky" without explanatory phrase complain because the addition of "neutral spirits" in the label takes away some of their trade, they are without a just ground, because they lose their trade merely from a statement of fact. The straight whisky men are relieved

Solicitor General Lloyd Bowers from the September 9, 1910 *Washington Times*, reproduced here. *Library of Congress.*

from all future attempts to pass of neutral spirits as straight whisky. More than this, if straight whisky or any other kind of whisky is aged in the wood, the fact may be branded on the package, and this claim to public favor may be truthfully put forth. Thus, the purpose of the Pure Food Law is fully accomplished in respect of misbranding and truthful branding.

The straight whiskey crowd thought the opinion did not go far enough, while most of the rectifiers thought it went too far. The foreign whiskey importers, including the owners of Canadian Club Whisky, were overjoyed.

Wiley reported that on the day Taft's opinion was released, he received a call from Bowers, who asked:

"Have you read the president's decision?" I said I have, "with great astonishment." He asked, "What do you think about it?" I replied, "I feel as if I had been spanked." To which he replied, "So do I." This was the last time I heard Lloyd Bowers's voice.

Some three weeks later, Bowers died, and in his 1929 book, Wiley said, "I think I was right in thinking that probably his premature death was due to a broken heart. Nobody was satisfied with the laborious efforts which he made."

In the final chapter of his book, Wiley provided:

> *Fortunately, the rectifiers did not have many years to enjoy the fruits of their great victory. The enactment of the Prohibition Amendment and the Volstead Act placed all dealings in beverage alcoholic drinks outside the law. The question now is not "What is whisky?" but "Where is whisky?" The adulterations of the bootleg brand are now more deadly than were the combinations of the rectifiers in the old days. These illegal decisions that permit alcohol to masquerade as whisky have never been repealed. They remain sonorous witnesses of the triumph of the unholy.*

Obviously, he never got over the rebuke.

SONS OF TEMPERANCE

The Sons of Temperance was founded in New York City on September 29, 1842, at a meeting at 71 Division Street. By 1870, there were more than five thousand divisions (each chapter was known as a division since the first meeting was held on Division Street) stretching across the country and into Canada, the United Kingdom and even Australia and New Zealand. As explained in an 1849 book on the order titled *An Address on the Order of the Sons of Temperance: Its History and Peculiar Advantages, with a Glance at the Principal Objections*:

1. *It is to all intents and purposes a* Temperance Society. *This is the primary design of the institution. All who enter its doors must, in a solemn manner, pledge their sacred honor as men, that they will: "neither make, buy, sell or use, as beverage, any spirituous or malt liquors, wine or cider." The members are constantly reminded of this solemn obligation whenever they listen to our beautiful and impressive ceremonies of initiation.*

2. *It possess the advantage of a* mutual health insurance company, *providing for its members in time of sickness. A fund is raised by the payment of a small initiation fee, which is fixed by the by-laws of each division—but which cannot be less than two dollars—and a regular due of not less than five cents per week or two dollars and sixty cents per annum.*

3. *It is a prominent feature of our organization to promote "brotherly love" among its members. Sons of Temperance meet in the division room, not merely for the transaction of ordinary business, but to use the language which sets forth the duties of that place, they meet to "propagate the principles of Temperance, Benevolence and Brotherly Love."*

According to article 3 of the order's Constitution for Subordinate Division, membership was limited to: "Persons, fourteen years of age and upwards, possessing a character for integrity and who have not been rejected by or expelled from any other division within [the last] six months." The order was highly regulated with a national division that was known as the "Supreme Power of the Order," with all the other divisions being called subordinate divisions. Each had separate constitutions, rules of order, codes of law and manuals of decisions. Each subordinate division followed a "manual of business" that provided the details of the officers' duties, ceremonies, rituals, songs, proper wearing of regalia and conduct of division meetings that took place behind closed doors. In every order book, the following text appeared:

The star represents the light which TEMPERANCE has shed upon the world in darkness—a pole star to the wandering and tempest-tossed, a morning star to a brighter day, one of the brightest luminaries in the constellation of virtues.

The triangle, in allusion to the unalterable truth of mathematical and geometrical figures and quantities, is intended to represent the cardinal principles of the order—

LOVE, PURITY AND FIDELITY.

LOVE, the inspiring motive to do good to all men and especially to the brotherhood; PURITY in heart and conduct and freedom from all base and selfish motives and views; and FIDELITY in redeeming every vow and pledge and in promoting the interest of the order in the world.

Each division had the following officers.

- worthy patriarch
- worthy associate
- recording scribe
- assistant recording scribe
- financial scribe
- treasurer
- chaplain
- conductor
- assistant conductor
- inside sentinel
- outside sentinel

Members were known as brothers, and each office had detailed requirements for the conduct of meetings and specific regalia, such as "crossed gavels" for the worthy patriarch, "crossed pens with scroll" for the recording scribe and "crossed swords" for the inside sentinel. At the national division, the titles were proceeded by "most" (for example: most worthy patriarch).

Almost from the beginning, the order was criticized for being a secret society, like the Masons or Odd Fellows. It even had a brother who quit the order and published an exposition on its inner workings. That former brother, Martin Stowell, wrote the following in his 1848 *An Exposition of the Secret Order of the Sons of Temperance with Facts in Relation to Secret Societies in General*:

> *The fact that the meetings of such societies are not public, when the institutions are so widespread over the country and the most foul plots can be laid against the government, against societies, as well as against the lives and properties of individuals; and that these schemes can be set on foot, spread over the country and everything made ready to carry them into effect and also to execute them, without comparatively any fear of being detected, is enough to arouse the thinking part of any community to action and to enlist every friend of universal brotherhood in an uncompromising warfare against such institutions. I think in Washington's farewell address to Congress he said, "Beware of secret societies."*

Stowell went on to say that the members of the order were "heathenish in the performance of their ceremonies." In laying out the details of the secrecy obligations that new brothers had to accept, he said that upon admittance, candidates were told to stand in a circle around the worthy patriarch and were required to undertake the following obligation, "I, [name], do solemnly pledge my sacred honor as a man, that I will never divulge any password explanation, ceremony or other private matter of the order, that I will never take or keep a copy of them or allow any other person so to do; that I will do all within my power to promote the interests of the order."

The order's password or phrase was changed every three months and was communicated to the entire order from the national division. No brother was allowed entrance into a division meeting without the current password. It was the duty of the outside sentinel to ensure the sanctity of meetings. The following is an excerpt from a description of how, according to Stowell, the initiation ceremony for a new brother was to be run:

The candidate was led around the room and placed in front of the worthy patriarch, who rose from his seat and said:

Who hath woes?
Who hath sorrow?
Who hath contentions?
Who hath wounds without cause?

In answer to each, the division members (standing behind the candidate) chant:

They that tarry long at the wine; they that seek strong drink.

The worthy patriarch then continued:

Then look not upon the wine, when it giveth its color in the cup, for, at last, it biteth like a serpent and stingeth like an adder.

The whole division then said, "Look not upon the wine," and the assistant conductor said, "Behold another who renounceth the wine and turneth away from strong drink."

The division responded in one voice, "Welcome, brother!"

The assistant conductor then said, "Yes, welcome, brother! And to what are thou welcome? To thine own good, to thine own felicity. It is here thou are safe from the all-pervading destroyer."

The assistant conductor then whispered, "Be merry, be sober," and then proffered the cup of enchantment. "Dash it down," responds the whole division. "Yes, dash it down," repeats the conductor and continues, "Touch but a drop, and behold the vast ocean surrounds thee, to sink and overwhelm thee forever."

In their fight against the secretive nature of the ceremonies, the order identified the ceremonies as being solemn and impressive and went on to state:

We are not acquainted with any composition which is more chaste and appropriate than that which is used in the services of our order; and there is

61

nothing in connection with these services which could be in the least offensive to the most sensitive mind or heart. On the contrary, they produce a happy effect upon the new member and never grow old or stale by familiarity. "But why not make them public, if they are so good?" Because they are our private property; because they would lose much of their effect upon the new member; and because thousands of young men (and sometimes old men) are brought to the order by curiosity, who are by this means saved from the all-pervading destroyer and made the fast friends of temperance.

***

There is only one class of men who have reason to apprehend any danger from the Sons of Temperance, as they are only class not represented among them—the rumseller and his allies. While we are bound to respect the rights of all, we would not ensure their "peculiar institution" against the operations of our order. We have our appropriate work—that work is to propagate the principles of temperance and benevolence; and those, only, who oppose these objects, need entertain any fears of this institution.

A book titled *Manual of Decisions of the National Division of the Sons of Temperance of North America* from 1878 states:

As members of society and as citizens, we have the right, and it is our duty to exercise it to suppress by all legitimate and honorable means the manufacture of and traffic in intoxicating drinks, and in becoming Sons of Temperance, we give up none of our moral rights and are exempt from none of our duties as citizens.

Drinking saloons in legislative capitols are injurious to public morals, preventative of pure legislation, disgraceful to public morals and should be immediately abolished.

Divisions Active in the District

In Washington, D.C., the Sons of Temperance had many active divisions operating from the 1850s until the early 1900s. On July 4, 1851, several Washington, D.C. divisions, along with divisions from Virginia and Maryland, received and welcomed the Grand Division of the Sons of Temperance of the State of Pennsylvania. The occasion was to present a memorial stone "for the noble and grand monument now erecting to the memory of Washington." There are 195 memorial stones inside the Washington Monument. They were presented by various organizations that were active when the memorial was being built between 1848 and 1884.

The program for the festivities of the Pennsylvania Division began with the procession of its members congregating at E and Seventh Streets, where they marched down to Pennsylvania Avenue and then turned west to the the monument grounds. Upon arrival, the Pennsylvania grand worthy patriarch introduced the Pennsylvania delegation, delivered an address and presented the stone to President Millard Fillmore, who was an ex-officio president of the Monumental Association.

The memorial stones are viewable on both elevator rides up and down the monument. The Sons of Temperance have seven stones: two on the 70-foot landing from the Grand Divisions of North Carolina and Virginia; one from the Grand Division of the State of Connecticut on the 90-foot landing; one from the State of Rhode Island Sons of Temperance on the 120-foot landing; one on the 180-foot landing from the State of Pennsylvania that reads, "The surest safeguard of the liberty of our country is Total Abstinence from all that intoxicates"; two on the 210-foot landing; one from the State of Illinois Sons of Temperance; and one from the Grand Division of Ohio.

The Pennsylvania Sons of Temperance Memorial Stone for the Washington Monument. *National Park Service.*

By 1876, there were at least eight divisions of the Sons of Temperance spread across the city, according to that year's city directory. They were:

- the Grand Division, which met quarterly at 433 Ninth Street Northwest.
- No. 1 Howard Division, which met on Wednesdays at Temperance Temple.
- No. 2 Columbia Division, which met on Tuesdays at Fourth and East Capitol Streets.
- No. 3 Equal Division, which met at the corner of Seventh Street and New York Avenue.
- No. 4 South Washington Division, which met on Mondays at Potomac Hall.
- No. 6 Rescue Division, which met on Tuesdays at Temperance Hall, located at 432 Ninth Street Northwest.
- No. 7 East Washington Division, which met on Saturdays at Baum's Hall at the corner of Fourth and East Capitol Streets Northeast.
- No. 11 Mount Pleasant Division, which met on Fridays at Union Hall in Mount Pleasant.

Taking a closer look at the Mount Pleasant Division and its effect on that specific suburb of the city, in a document titled "The Annals of Mount Pleasant" that was produced in July 1876 as part of the centennial celebration of the Fourth of July, there is a curious passage that reads:

> *In the spring of 1875, the Mount Pleasant Division Sons of Temperance was organized…and at one time embraced nearly every person in the village. Its first presiding officer was* [Harvey] *H.C. Harmon, and it is still in a flourishing condition.*

In the September 27, 1879 edition of the *Washington Evening Star*, a letter of "correspondence" from Mount Pleasant (described as "the region of the heights north of Boundary Street [Florida Avenue] and centering on Fourteenth Street") reads:

> *As there are probably many persons living within the limits of the District who are not acquainted with the beautiful suburban village of Mount Pleasant, a short letter of description may prove interesting…The villagers*

are mostly government employees and nearly all New England people. Many of the villagers raise their own poultry, keep their cattle, have a garden and produce their own vegetables and keep a neat flower garden, while some possess fine fruit orchards. There are two good stores in the village, which supply the necessaries of everyday life....

The village has a neatly built hall containing three rooms, which is used for church services, Sabbath school, debating clubs, the Temperance Order and balls and parties. The main room will accommodate about 150 people....

During the winter, the villagers have a continual round of festivities, which include minstrel entertainments by an organization in the village known as the "Tropical Exotics," balls, parties and soirees, entertainments by the Temperance Order....

The fact that there is no spirituous liquor sold in the village betokens a temperate, industrious and thrifty little settlement where there is little sickness, few deaths, quiet nights and pure atmosphere to breathe unfreighted with the nauseous gases of asphalt nuisances which make life bitter for city people.

The hall mentioned in the previous quote was called the Union Hall but was sometimes called the Union Temperance Hall or the Mount Pleasant Opera House (it was located where 1520–26 Newton Street is today). It is interesting that four of our liquor merchants chose to make "dry" Mount Pleasant their home.

Lemonade Lucy

Rescue Division No. 6 of the Sons of Temperance played a prominent role in a temperance controversy concerning First Lady Lucy Webb "Lemonade Lucy" Hayes in 1878. On the occasion of the first major social event of President Rutherford B. Hayes's administration, the April 19, 1877 state dinner held in honor of the Grand Duke Alexei of Russia and his companion Grand Duke Konstantin, a "full quota of wine" was served as it always was during previous administrations. But afterward, President and Mrs. Hayes announced that no alcohol of any kind would be served in the White House. Mrs. Hayes was raised by a grandfather who was a lifelong adherent to the temperance movement, and his influence was evident, as she was an opponent of alcohol in any form. As the first first lady to earn a college degree (from Cincinnati Wesleyan Female College), she penned an essay as an undergrad titled "Has Society a Right to Prohibit the Manufacture and Sale of Ardent Spirits?" Her husband, the president, was known to not mind a drink here or there, but he decided to try to court the temperance advocates by going in on the ban in the White House. In fact, President Hayes was listed as a member of the Sons of Temperance.

In announcing the ban, Mrs. Hayes was quoted as saying, "I have sons who have never tasted liquor. They shall not receive from my hand, or with the sanction that its use in the family would give, the first taste of what might prove their ruin. What I wish for my own sons, I must do for other mothers." The liquor ban in the White House did not go over well with the politicians and journalists who were accustomed to having alcohol at White House functions. But temperance organizations like the Woman's Christian Temperance Union (WCTU) trumpeted the ban. WCTU's president Frances Willard boasted of Hayes, "By the example of such leaders, temperance will become the fashion." In temperance circles, Mrs. Hayes was a hit—so much so that a Washington-based temperance organization decided to name itself the Mrs. R.B. Hayes Temperance Society.

The fame turned out to be short-lived; according to an April 29, 1878 *Washington Post* article, that named society decided to repudiate its name due to an alleged comment attributed to Mrs. Hayes while she was on a trip to a Philadelphia event where claret was served. Apparently, she, in not objecting to the wine being served, said:

> *It is a great mistake to suppose I desire to dictate my views to others in this matter of the use of wine and such drinks. I do not use them myself or in my family, but I have no thought of shunning those who think differently; it is a mistake to think that I should want to be so dictatorial. I want people to enjoy themselves in the manner most pleasing to them.*

Thinking that the first lady was not dedicated to the temperance effort, based on the incident and her alleged comments, the head of the Mrs. R.B. Hayes Temperance Society rejected her as a fraud and disavowed the society's name. Other temperance organizations stepped in to defend Mrs. Hayes. In a May 2, 1878 *Washington Post* article titled "A Tribute to Mrs. Hayes: The Action of Rescue Division, No. 6 Sons of Temperance," it was reported that this group had adopted a preamble and a series of resolutions that such an influence as Mrs. Hayes:

PLAN ACTIVE WORK

Program of the District Sons of Temperance.

TWO DIVISIONS FORMED

Open-Air Meetings, Countryside Rallies and Series of Entertainments in View.

JOHN C. FOSTER,
Reorganizer Sons of Temperance.

The recently reorganized Sons of Temperance organization is planning for a spring and summer campaign with the view of gaining a large increase in membership. Open-air meetings will be held and countryside rallies, besides entertainments and outings. Past Patriarch John C. Foster is taking a leading part in the movement, which was inaugurated Friday night with an open meeting under the auspices of Columbia Division, No. 2.

The program was carried out under the direction of the committee. The first number was a recitation, "Moses Before Pharaoh," by Mr. Boynton, who was liberally applauded, and as an encore he recited "The Last Day of School."

John C. Foster, the reorganizer of the Sons of Temperance from the April 3, 1910 *Washington Evening Star*, reproduced here. *Library of Congress.*

Is needed in the capital of the nation, in the nursery, in the church and in society, that "God forgive her" should be said for every lady who places the intoxicating cup before her guests that the society resolutions, reflecting upon Mrs. Hayes, were in the interest of the liquor dealers and against the temperance cause and an influential worker therein and that the authors of the resolutions are branded as shallow-brained, God-forsaken slanderers, their report false, malicious and cowardly and that Mrs. Hayes is fully exonerated from all such slanderous allegations.

That the trite nickname for Hayes has stuck belies the facts that she was actually a witty, well-educated and warm-hearted woman who raised the prestige of the first lady in American life.

An April 1, 1896 article in the *Washington Post* titled "An Old Order Revived—Sons of Temperance Re-Established in Washington" provided that the temperance society, though very prominent during the late war, had all "but died almost completely out in the District about ten years ago." Likely part of what helped kill the organization was an 1894 decree from the pope that forbade Catholics from belonging to the Knights of Pythias, Odd Fellows or the Sons of Temperance. As reported in the December 31, 1894 edition of the *Washington Post*, the substance of the decree was that:

Members of the societies will not be excommunicated but will be deprived of their right or receiving the sacraments of the church. The reason for issuing the decree was that the societies had a tendency to make their members worldly and cause them to be lax in their religious duties.

The decree was later modified in 1896 to allow Catholics who had belonged to targeted organizations before the publication of the original decree "to leave their names upon the rolls of those societies and to pay into the treasury dues and assessments whenever pecuniary loss and detriment would follow from complete severance of ties." However, the general prohibition from Catholics' participation in any proceedings of the societies remained.

By 1909, most of the Sons of Temperance divisions in Washington had again died out. When John C. Foster sought to reestablish the organization, all that was left was the grand lodge charter and the grand worthy patriarch F.M. Bradley. In an event described in an April 3, 1910 *Evening Star* article, both Washington Division No. 1 and Columbia Division No. 2 were reconstituted with new members who had a plan to organize a new division in Clarendon, Virginia. In remarks at the event, Mr. Bradley said:

> *The misery on Earth is caused by the acts of man, and that if everyone would join the temperance cause by becoming a member of the Sons of Temperance and putting his energy in that direction instead of letting it go to waste, "this would be a beautiful, bountiful world for those who through the curse of alcohol now see only the darkest side."*

PART II

THE WHISKEY
PRODUCERS

6

WILLIAM D. BARRY

MOUNT PLEASANT CLUB WHISKEY

*T*he bottle that started this project was found by the previous owner of my house during a renovation in the 1980s. It was found under some roof shingles. The bottle is a small rectangular druggist bottle that was made in the shape commonly known as the "Blake" style. The Blake was a standard offering of most glassmakers that produced druggist bottles from the 1880s well into the 1920s.

Barry owned the Reliable Family Liquor Store located at 2024 Fourteenth Street Northwest between 1907 and 1911. Located on the west side of Fourteenth Street, just north of U Street, the Frank D. Reeves Center for Municipal Affairs City Government office building now occupies the spot. The house where the bottle was found on Nineteenth Street in Mount Pleasant was finished and offered for sale in June 1911, which suggests that the workers who built the house left the bottle behind after they were done.

Apparently, it was a tradition for workers to leave behind an empty bottle of whatever the crew drank upon the completion of a job. Indeed, the bottles from a few of the liquor merchants covered later in this book were found in rowhouses (McGuire's Federal Seal, Drury's Haviland Rye and Morris' Westover Rye).

This page: Photographs of the Mount Pleasant Club Whiskey bottle. *Jason Hamacher*.

An N.L. Sansbury Real Estate advertisement from the June 10, 1911 *Washington Evening Star*, reproduced here. *Washington, D.C. Public Library.*

Patrick F. Neligan

It turns out that Barry wasn't the original purveyor of Mount Pleasant Club Whiskey. The brand was sold at the same store prior to Barry's arrival on the scene. Indeed, many Blake-style bottles have been found in the area embossed with the name "P.F. Neligan" instead of Barry's followed by "Reliable Family Liquor Store." Unfortunately, none have been found with the label still intact. We do know that Patrick F. Neligan owned the store at least as early as 1905. No documentary evidence of Mount Pleasant Club Whiskey existing before 1905 has been found, but it is possible that it was sold by Neligan prior to the advertisement being placed in the *Washington Post*—just how early it was sold will remain a mystery for now.

In addition to selling liquor, Neligan was a property developer. As early as 1901, there are records of him buying and selling properties in and around the Shaw and Eckington neighborhoods, including much of the northwest corner of Fourteenth and U Streets. For example, according to a June 10, 1906 article from the *Evening Star*, he sold 2008 Fourteenth Street Northwest to the North Savings Bank for $12 per square foot in cash. The bank was to temporarily remodel the existing building for bank business and would later build a ten-story building on the site. In a May 9, 1909 *Evening Star* article, it was reported that Neligan bought 2010 Fourteenth Street, a building with three stories and a cellar with a large storefront on the first floor and dwelling apartments above for the price of $15,500, representing a value of $3.60 per square foot. The lot had a frontage of 20 feet and a depth of 138 feet, containing 2,770 square feet of land. The article mentions that the area's "recent marked development into a business section" was the result of the Capital Traction Company Street railway line connecting its Fourteenth Street line to its U Street line, with the latter terminating at Union Station.

Neligan also owned a grocery store at 1908–10 Fourteenth Street (just south of U Street). A March 17, 1913 *Evening Star* advertisement states:

EAT RIGHT, DRINK RIGHT
The best the market affords in eatables and drinkables is exactly for your table and sideboard.
GROCERIES, WINES, LIQUORS
This $20,000 Wine Cellar Is a Wonder.

John C. Long of 1908 Fifteenth Street Northwest won a jingle contest in late 1907 after penning the following for Neligan's store: "For all things good

P. F. NELIGAN

Imported and Domestic

WINES, WHISKIES,
BEER, GINGER ALE
and
MINERAL WATERS

Established 22 Years

1908 14th Street N. W.

Washington D. C.

WM. D. BARRY

Highest Grades of

Family Wines and Liquors

BUDWEISER AND SCHLITZ BEERS
ON DRAUGHT

MT. PLEASANT CLUB
Vatted and Blended Whiskey

TELEPHONE NORTH 757   BUFFET IN REAR

2008 14th Street N. W.
WASHINGTON, D. C.

Left: A P.F. Neligan advertisement from the August 28, 1915 *Washington Herald*, reproduced here. *Library of Congress*.

Right: A William D. Barry advertisement from the August 28, 1915 *Washington Herald*, reproduced here. *Library of Congress*.

in the grocery line / Coffee, tea, fruits, spices and wines / There is not a store that can compete / With P.F. Neligan 1908 Fourteenth Street."

Interestingly, in the December 24, 1913 edition of the *Evening Star*, it was reported that Barry had received approval from the Excise Board (more on them later) to transfer his liquor license from 2024 to 2008 Fourteenth Street, where the bank had been located. In a 1915 advertisement, Neligan professed he had been in business for twenty-two years. Could he have sold Mount Pleasant Club Whiskey as early as 1893? On the same page of the newspaper that contained Neligan's advertisement, Barry also ran an advertisement.

"RECOMMENDED BY PHYSICIANS"

Like almost every other pre-Prohibition whiskey out there, Mount Pleasant Club Whiskey touted its medicinal properties in its advertisements, and the label even stated that it was "Recommended by Physicians." Since ancient times, there have been widespread beliefs that alcoholic beverages have medicinal value. Historian W.J. Rorabaugh wrote in his 1979 book *The Alcoholic Republic*:

Americans in the early eighteenth century classified whiskey, rum and other liquors as medications that could cure colds, fevers, snakebites, frosted toes and broken legs and as relaxants that would relieve depression, reduce tension and enable hardworking laborers to enjoy a moment of happy frivolous camaraderie.

It wasn't until 1916 that whiskey and brandy were removed from the list of scientifically approved medicines in *The Pharmacopeia of the United States of America*. The American Medical Association passed a resolution in 1917, after a contentious vote, that read:

Whereas, we believe that the use of alcohol is detrimental to the human economy and,

Whereas, its use in therapeutics as a tonic or stimulant or food has no scientific value, therefore,

Be it Resolved, that the American Medical Association is opposed to the use of alcohol as a beverage; and:

Be it Further Resolved, that the use of alcohol as a therapeutic agent should be further discouraged.

Prior to this resolution and until Prohibition, the alcohol industry made pretty much every claim possible about the medicinal effects of liquor. Each of the early whiskey makers covered in this book made extraordinary claims about the medicinal properties of their respective whiskeys.

Neligan's May 14, 1905 advertisement for Mount Pleasant Club Whiskey stated:

To Cure a Cold

This is the season when an epidemic of colds is prevalent. One of the best remedies for the ordinary cold is a wine glass of our Mount Pleasant Club Whiskey diluted with some hot water, the juice of a lemon and some quinine. Take when going to bed. Our line of imported wines and whiskeys is a good as any in the northwest. Our facilities for supplying the family trade are exceptional. Orders delivered immediately. Our special Mount Pleasant Club Whiskey, $1.00 the quart. P.F. Neligan, 2024 Fourteenth [Street]. Phone, North 757.

It turns out that quinine and its use with whiskey has quite a history. Westerners (Spanish conquistadors) in the 1570s in what is now Peru discovered that the ground bark of cinchona trees had antifebrile properties and could be mixed with drinks like wine. Cinchona is also known to have been used to treat fevers in Rome in the 1630s. Rome had long suffered malarial epidemics, killing popes, cardinals, bishops and countless others. By 1677, cinchona was listed in the *London Pharmacopoeia*. Quinine was isolated from the cinchona bark in 1820 by two French researchers, Pierre-Joseph Pelletier and Joseph Caventou.

By 1850, the use of quinine to fight fevers from malaria and other diseases was common around the world. In the United States, a Missouri physician, John Sappington, MD, was responsible for much of its widespread use. After Sappington experimented by taking some quinine himself in 1823, he used his enslaved people to manufacture pills that were sold all over the country. He wrote a book called *The Theory and Treatments of Fevers* in 1844 that included his formula alongside patient testimonials.

When the Civil War started, doctors had very few effective medicines. The "miracle" medicines were morphine, ether, chloroform and quinine. In a 1906 article titled "The Use of Quinine During the Civil War," physician John W. Churchman, MD, listed the "sinews" of the war: coffee,

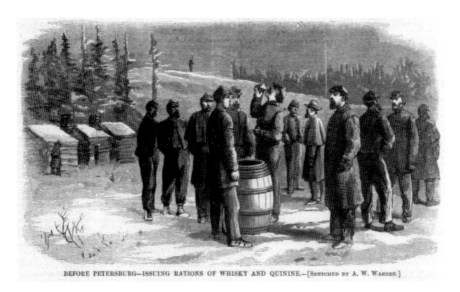

BEFORE PETERSBURG—ISSUING RATIONS OF WHISKY AND QUININE.—[Sketched by A. W. Warren.]

Union troops being given their doses of quinine and whiskey during the Petersburg Campaign. Andrew W. Warren was an artist from *Harper's Weekly* who traveled with the Army of the Potomac during the campaign. *From* Harper's Weekly, *March 11, 1865, reproduced here.*

cathartics, ammunition, whiskey and quinine. Quinine was found to be quite effective, as Union troops experienced the southern climate and disease during the war.

Barrels of whiskey, to which the required amount of quinine had been added, were prepared by Union stewards, and each troop was administered a dose each morning. Union troops were also given doses of quinine and whiskey during the Petersburg Campaign. Andrew W. Warren was an artist from *Harper's Weekly* who traveled with the Army of the Potomac during the campaign.

The practice was so common in the army that songs were written about "quinine call" or "Q-call." The practice fell out of favor, however, due to the taste of the mixture, so quinine doses were then limited to soldiers who exhibited the early symptoms of fever. A popular jingle illustrating that rye whiskey and quinine was a visible and well known cure for "la grippe," also known as influenza, in popular culture, was captured by a Baltimore resident named Meredith Janvier:

> *Little grains of quinine, little drops of rye*
> *Make la grippe that's got you drop its head and fly*
> *This will quickly help you if you'll only try,*
> *But when you take the quinine, don't forget the rye.*

An article from the December 31, 1907 edition of the *Evening Star* titled "Whisky and Quinine: Herman George Gets Thirty Days for Assault" shows that whiskey and quinine were considered a common remedy for the "grip" (influenza). In this particular case, it appears that Mr. George got the wrong balance of the two components:

> *Herman George, a laborer, was sent to jail for thirty days today in default of a $10 fine for assaulting Timmie McFarland, a newsboy, at Pennsylvania avenue and Ninth Street yesterday afternoon. Policeman Groff of the first precinct station testified he saw the accused first knock a small girl over, then cross the street and assault the boy. The child was badly bruised, and a large bundle of papers [was] thrown into the mud and made unsalable.*
> *"What was the trouble?" asked Judge Kimball, as the prisoner took the stand in his own behalf. "Whisky and quinine for the grip," answered George. "Too bad, too bad," replied the court. The pharmaceutical compound was evidently not properly balanced. Guilty.*

A closer look at the court case, *United States v. 10 Cases of Quinine Whisky*, illustrates how enforcement of Section 8 of the Pure Food and Drug Act of 1906 began to put a stop to such claims about the magical medicinal qualities of whiskey. In this case, ten cases of twelve bottles were siezed because the bottles were labeled "Quinine Whisky" and contained the following statements, "Contains Pure Quinine," "the greatest preventative and remedy for all malarial complaints ever offered," "prevents and cures a cold," "the greatest tonic for convalescents from typhus and typhoid fever" and "an infallible cure for la grippe." In his opinion, Judge Landis found that the bottles were misbranded in violation of Section 8 of the Food and Drug Act:

> The labels appearing upon the cases, cardboard cartons and bottles containing the aforesaid drug, to wit, quinine whisky, bear statements which are false and misleading in that the labels attached to each bottle declare that the drug contains pure quinine…where, in truth and in fact, the drug does not contain quinine in the quantity stated upon the label; and that it is further misbranded in that the labels…bear no statement of alcoholic content of the aforesaid product. And the court further finds that the aforesaid drug, to wit, quinine whisky was further misbranded in that the labels attached to the cases, cartons and bottles containing said drug bore statements concerning the qualities and ingredients of the aforesaid product which were false and misleading and calculated to deceive purchasers.

Knowing that their whiskey could be seized if it contained such statements, whiskey producers changed the way they advertised their products.

WHY THE "CLUB" IN WHISKEY?

The enterprising American turned Canadian who we met in part one, Hiram Walker, the founder of Canadian Club, is the one to thank for all the whiskeys that have the word *club* in their names. Walker picked a bad time to start distilling whiskey in Detroit, as the State of Michigan adopted Prohibition the following year, 1855. As Walker was starting out in business, there were already a number of dry states: Vermont (1850), Illinois (1851), Connecticut (1854) and Delaware, Indiana and Nebraska (1855). Undeterred by the advent of Prohibition in Michigan, Walker simply moved his operation across the Detroit River to Canada in a place that eventually became known as Walkerville.

In the 1860s, Walker's whiskeys were available only at gentlemen's clubs across the Midwest in cities like Detroit, Chicago and Cincinnati. This availability led to membership spikes at these establishments. To capitalize on the demand, he changed the name of his whiskey to "club whisky," since his whiskey could be found only at these clubs. Thus, he became the first distiller to brand his whiskey "club whisky," and the trend caught on.

As Walker's whiskey became more popular, it began to make inroads into the markets of the Northeast, Midwest and mid-Atlantic. American distillers started to get angry that a Canadian whiskey had gained such market presence—essentially, in their eyes, stealing their business. So, they successfully lobbied Congress to pass a law in 1880 requiring all foreign spirits to clearly state their country of origin on the label. This backfired spectacularly, however, in the case of the whiskey from our northern neighbor. Initially, in order to comply with the law, Walker just put the word *Canadian* on a small ring on the neck of the bottle. The public, fearing that the law would make "imported" liquor harder to obtain, started to hoard it. Demand skyrocketed—so much that in 1889, Walker decided to reposition "Canadian" to be on his bottles' main label next to "Club." The genius move worked, and everyone began calling his whiskey Canadian Club.

In addition to Mount Pleasant Club Whiskey and Columbia Club, the following are a few other "club" whiskeys that were advertised contemporaneously in Washington newspapers: Maryland Club Whiskey, Somerset Club Whiskey, Murray Hill Club Whiskey, Millionaires' Club Whiskey, Metropolitan Club Whiskey, Windsor Club Whiskey and Lexington Club Whiskey. Obviously, the actual "clubs" were left behind.

BARRY'S PART IN THE FIGHT TO KEEP THE DISTRICT WET

In addition to selling liquor, Barry played a prominent role in the ultimately losing fight to keep the teetotalers out of the city. In an article in the September 20, 1907 edition of the *Evening Star*, Barry was identified as one of the three members appointed to a committee of the Retail Liquor Dealers' Association of Washington, D.C., to bring all workers involved in liquor or beer production and sales together to contest the growing influence of the temperance movement.

WANT THIS TO BE A "DRY TOWN"
STEPS TO BRING ABOUT PROHIBITION
IN THE DISTRICT
Determined Effort Will be Made by Temperance Advocates, Plans
of Liquor Dealers

A most determined effort to bring about Prohibition in the District of Columbia will be made this winter, according to several leading temperance advocates. As the cold season approaches, they say, there will be an amalgamation of all the cold water forces and many of the churches in Washington in order that the movement may be concerted.

***

The [liquor men's] *committee was appointed to bring about an affiliation of all liquor interests in the District of Columbia, aggregating it was said, about 18,000 men.*

It is understood the committee will confer with the following organizations, with a view of forming a confederation: Brewers, Brewery Workers, Beer Drivers, Bartenders' Union, Cigarmakers' Union, Cigar Manufacturers' Association, Beer Bottlers' Association, Wholesale Liquor Dealers' Association and the Drummers' Assocaiton of the Wholesale Liquor Trade. It was stated that the members of these assocations mentioned represent approximately 40,000 persons.

"It is our purpose to concentrate our forces to meet the assault of the prohibitionist," a member of the committee explained.

THE DISTRICT'S 1913 EXCISE LAW
AND THE ANTI-SALOON LEAGUE

The temperance movement succeeded in having the Jones-Works Excise Liquor Law of the District of Columbia go into effect on July 1, 2013. Some of the features of the new law, as reported in the March 2, 1913 *Evening Star*, were:

- *A new Excise Board was to be appointed by the president.*
- *Not more than four saloons on a block and no more than three on one side of the street.*

- *No saloons in residence districts or within one mile of the Soldiers' Home, or within 300 feet of residence alley, or within 400 feet of a public school or college, or 400 feet of established house of religious worship.*
- *Sales limited between the hours of 7 a.m. and midnight.*
- *Pool and billiards forbidden in saloons, except hotels and clubs, and music, except in clubs, hotels or restaurants.*
- *Free lunches and growlers now prohibited.*

Having a new Excise Board to administer the rules and regulations of the liquor trade was seen by the temperance forces to be important, as they felt the old board had been inefficient and lax. The Anti-Saloon League played a prominent role in getting this law passed. The motto of the Anti-Saloon League was, "The saloon must go." And the organization used "all means deemed honorable and expedient to accomplish that purpose." One of the organizations leaders was attorney A.E. Shoemaker.

In the lead-up to the law's passage, the arguments of temperance advocates and the liquor interests about how stringent the regulations needed to be were debated in public. An editorial titled "What Liquor Legislation the District Needs and Why" from the May 13, 1912 edition of the *Washington Times* argued that, with a population of 331,000, 513 licensed saloons were too many, stating that a better number would be 331 (the final law landed on 300), which equals 1 saloon for each 1,000 persons.

The editorial, in arguing against "a certain class of hotels," noted:

> *Whatever the liquor dealers' association has done to clean up saloons, they have either not tried or else trying have not succeeded in cleaning up hotels. IT IS PROBABLY TRUE THAT THERE IS NOT A CITY IN THE COUNTRY A MORE THREATENING SOURCE OF EVIL THAN A CERTAN CLASS OF HOTEL IN WASHINGTON. What could be a more efficient emissary of the devil than a reputable hotel which renders its rooms attractive with decorations and lights, with visible allurements and attractions, then allows it to be understood that the purchase of food there means THAT LIQUOR WILL BE SERVED WITHOUT QUESTION TO MINORS AND THEIR COMPANIONS? It isn't that the evil stops with the drinking of liquors; it is what is likely to follow in ruined girls and debauched boys. And yet, if that hotel's proprietor was hauled into court, his lawyer would contend that his client had the required number of rooms and must be allowed to*

sell liquor, and the judge would declare, "So sayeth the law." The EXCISE BOARD OUGHT NOT TO HAVE TO CONVICT A HOTEL KEEPER IF HIS HOUSE BEARS A DISREPUTABLE NAME. ITS GENERAL REPUTATION BEING BAD, IT OUGHT TO BE PUT OUT OF BUSINESS.

The first sentence of the preceding quote refers to efforts by Barry, as president of the Federation of Retail Liquor Dealers of D.C., to institute industry self-regulation instead of Excise Board regulation. The following is an excerpt from a letter Barry penned to the Excise Board in 1909 that provided a declaration of principles for his retailers to follow:

The duties of the retail liquor dealers are:

- *To obey all ordinances.*
- *To obey all orders of the Excise Board.*
- *To faithfully obey the letter and spirit of the Sunday closing law.*
- *To refuse to sell liquor to any intoxicated person or to any known inebriate or minor.*
- *To limit the giving of free lunch to crackers, cheese and pretzels and nothing else.*
- *To prohibit the serving of drinks to any female to be drank at any public bar.*
- *To oppose the employment of any female for the purpose of dispensing liquor.*
- *To prevent gambling in any and all forms upon the premise.*
- *To conduct your place of business that your neighbors will feel that it is a necessity to the neighborhood.*
- *To look to the deportment of your employees in or about your place of business and see that at all times, they conduct themselves properly and never appear under the influence of liquor.*
- *To stop the sale of five-cent growlers and limit the sale of beer in buckets to residents of the immediate neighborhood; and not to sell or give beer in a bucket to drivers of teams and vehicles to be drank upon the street.*
- *To prevent disorderly conduct and indecent language in or about your place of business, as well as loafing of disorderly persons in or about the place.*
- *To exclude from all saloons and public bars all indecent pictures and cards and to discourage the use of indecent pictures or labels for*

advertising purposes by the makers of or dealers in liquor, or cigars, or cigarettes, or other goods handled by saloons.

- *To regard and treat all fellow liquor dealers who violate these rules of conduct as detrimental to the best interest of the liquor trade.*

Apparently, these rules of conduct made a difference in the retail trade but not with the hotels.

When it came time to pick new members for the Excise Board, the temperance advocates were vocal in who they supported. The liquor dealers, on the other hand, were reticent to put forward anyone. In a March 23, 1913 *Evening Star* article, Barry denied a rumor that the liquor interests had named three men to fill the positions:

Advocacy Held Unwise

The sentiment of those liquor dealers who were talked to last night was that it would be very unwise for them to advocate any persons for the board, as this would mean certain defeat. William D. Barry of 2024 Fourteenth Street Northwest, president of the Retail Liquor Dealers' Association of the District, disclaimed any knowledge of action on the part of any of the liquor dealers. He declared his belief that the dealers should abide by the decision not to mix in the matter at all. He seemed to think that the dealers cared for nothing more than persons on the board who were taxpayers in the District and were known to be broad-minded and fair men.

On February 1, 1916, one hundred delegates from all the "wet" states met in Washington at the twenty-third annual conference of the National Retail Liquor Dealers' Association. It would be one of their last for quite some time. The *Evening Star* reported, "Liquor Men Begin Their Conference—Resolutions Will Be Considered Tomorrow, Expressing Associations Attitude on Sheppard Bill." At the conference, Barry was appointed to be on yet another committee, this time, the Congressional Committee. Unfortunately, Barry and his fellow committee members would have very little time to influence Congress, especially as it affected the liquor trade in Washington, as the "act to prevent the manufacture and sale of alcoholic liquors in the District of Columbia and for other purposes," known as the Sheppard Bone-Dry Act, was signed into law by President Woodrow Wilson on March 3, 1917. As a result, Washington went dry at midnight on November 1, 1917.

Morris Sheppard, the East Texas senator known as the "father of Prohibition," had used Washington as a testing ground for the criminalization of alcohol. Following the passage of the Bone-Dry Act, he went on to introduce the Eighteenth Amendment, and with its passage, he ushered in Prohibition for the entire country. Once the law was passed, he was so sure that his legislation wouldn't be overturned that he reportedly said, "There is as much of a chance of repealing the Eighteenth Amendment as there is for a hummingbird to fly to the planet Mars with the Washington Monument tied to its tail." Senator Sheppard remained in Washington after the passage of the Bone-Dry Act to monitor a legal claim aimed at overturning his Prohibition law. The effort failed, and prior to his departure for Texas, he had a few things to say about his new law:

> *The law providing Prohibition for the District of Columbia is one of the greatest steps forward in the interest of civilization, efficiency and happiness of the people of the District that could be possibly taken.*
>
> *Under the Prohibition law, it will be impossible for the Department of Labor in the future to make such a report as it recently made, showing that many of the poorer families here had a deficit charged to their accounts when their income and expenditures for the year were cast up. When the laboring man can no longer spend his money for whisky and beer at the corner saloon, conditions will be materially modified.*
>
> *There will be much more money available for the actual necessities of life and the proper maintenance of the family.*
>
> *The family income will be increased, for the workingman will do more regular and more efficient work.*
>
> *Prohibition means an immense gain to legitimate business in the District. Money which has hitherto been used for the purchase of liquor will now go into other channels of business.*
>
> *It means more comfort and enjoyment for the women and children.*
>
> *It will help to make Washington the capital of the nation, a model city, not only for the United States but for the whole world, as it should be. It will have a splendid effect upon the progress of Prohibition, both here and abroad.*
>
> *Prohibition is a step upward and forward for all the people of the District and particularly to those now connected with the liquor traffic.*

On the eve of Prohibition in Washington, D.C., the *Washington Post* reported that every policeman would be on duty and that officials "expected a very busy evening—during which, anything might happen." The officer in charge of the force issued an edict "that boisterous individuals are to be clapped into the lock-up. Intoxicated persons won't have their freedom long if they roam the street." It was also reported that many saloons had already exhausted their supply of liquor and that a number of them had been picked clean of their costly bar fixtures by saloon men from Baltimore, New York and Philadelphia. There were also many sales of "case goods," liquor sold by the case, reported, with the note that this indicated "that the holiday season won't pass by without proper accompaniments in many Washington homes."

The District branch of the police court was prepared for a night session to handle the expected deluge of cases, but the session was called off, with Judge Alexander R. Mullowny stating:

> [H]e did not feel there would be need for it. There were hardly more than fifteen persons in court today on charges of intoxication and that court said he did not believe that there would be any more than that number of charges tomorrow. Judge Mullowny said that the majority of saloonkeepers have disposed of their stocks and there would not be much intoxicants to be had tonight.
>
> Several men who were before the court today on charges of intoxication were told by Judge Mullowny that after today, he does not intend to be as lenient as he has been. With Prohibition in effect here, a man cannot come before me and say he did not intend to get drunk. There will be no unintentional drunks. For a man to get drunk now, he will first have to hunt for the intoxicants.

Such is Senator Morris Sheppard's legacy that, in 2014, a speakeasy called the Sheppard, in honor of the father of Prohibition, opened in Dupont Circle. In June 2021, the proprietors of the bar opened another speakeasy, which goes by the acronym OKPB, located on Mount Pleasant Street in the historically dry suburb Mount Pleasant.

BARRY'S LAST STORE AND "MERIDIAN HILL"

William Barry died at the age of seventy-two on August 27, 1936, in his house on Fairmont Street in Columbia Heights, a few blocks away from Mount Pleasant. His funeral mass was held at St. Paul's Catholic Church,

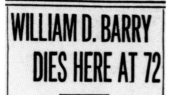

Was Banker and Business Man in District for Many Years.

William D. Barry, 1455 Fairmont street, banker and business man here for many years, died in Providence Hospital yesterday after a year's ill health. He was 72.

Mr. Barry was first vice-president of the United States Savings Bank for about 20 years before its closing in 1932 and was a director and stockholder before attaining that position.

During most of his life he was a liquor merchant, owning a store on Fourteenth street at the time of his death.

Mr. Barry was born in Williamsport, Md, coming here as a youth. He was a member of the Elks and the Holy Name Society. He attended St. Paul's Catholic Church.

He is survived by his widow, Mrs. Catherine C. Barry; two sons, William R. Barry and John E. Barry, all of Washington, and a sister, Mrs. Mary B. Clark, Euclid, Ohio. He had four grandchildren.

Funeral services will be held at his home at 9:30 a.m. tomorrow and at St. Paul's at 10. Burial will be in Mount Olivet Cemetery.

William D. Barry's obituary picture from the August 28, 1936 *Washington Evening Star*, reproduced here. *Library of Congress.*

and he was buried in the Mount Olivet Cemetery. He became a banker during Prohibition, acting as the first vice-president of the United States Savings Bank. The bank failed in 1932, and he returned to the liquor trade after Prohibition's repeal in 1933. His last store, Barry's Liquors, was located just a few doors down from his original store at 2016 Fourteenth Street Northwest. There is evidence in the form of a draft label that Barry sought to bring back Mount Pleasant Club Whiskey after Prohibition's repeal. The label, provided by Barry's great-grandson, states:

> *Mount Pleasant Club*
> *100 Proof*
> *Whiskey*
> *A Blend*
>
> *BOTTLED BY*
> *W. G. Bond, Inc. 30 Light St., Baltimore, Md.*
> *Exclusively for*
> *WM. D. BARRY*
> *2016 FOURTEENTH STREET, N.W.*
> *WASHINGTON, D.C.*

A November 11, 1933 advertisement from the *Baltimore Sun*, announcing the opening of W.G. Bond Inc. with its selection of ryes and gins, notes that Bond was the successor to the former firm Lamdin, Thompson and Co. that went under during Prohibition. W. Grayson Bond had an interest in that firm, and it may have provided the rye that was used to make the Barry's pre-Prohibition Mount Pleasant Club Whiskey. The following is a depiction of another bottle concept that Barry had for his post-repeal store, where the "club" was dropped from the label.

Left: An artist's rendition of a Mount Pleasant Whiskey bottle. *Courtesy of Ray Barry, the great-grandson of William D. Barry; from Christina Owens Knapp.*

Below: A William D. Barry advertisement in the *Washington Gaily News*. *Courtesy of Ray Barry, the great-grandson of William Barry.*

At the time of his death, Barry had a number of trademark applications for some of the liquor he was selling at his store. One in particular, "Meridian Hill," was for a whiskey or gin and was registered on April 9, 1935. The advertisement on the previous page indicates that the Meridian Hill Barry offered was likely a whiskey, given that it's listed as being "90 Proof." Meridian Hill was the name of a mansion located near the present-day intersection of Sixteenth and W Streets that was once the home of former president John Quincy Adams. It was so named because it was located on the exact longitude of the original District of Columbia milestone that was placed on April 15, 1791, placing it directly in the middle of the area set aside to become the District of Columbia. The U.S. government purchased the twelve-acre site in 1910 and created an Italian-style landscape of lawns, shaded walkways and gardens that is dotted with statuary, and it was officially opened in 1936. The park also contains one of the longest cascading fountains in North America. Located in the Columbia Heights neighborhood, adjacent to Mount Pleasant, it is right in the middle between where Barry lived, a few blocks north on the 1400 block of Fairmont Street, and his store to south on Fourteenth Street, near the intersection of U Street.

Though it is officially known as Meridian Hill Park by the National Park Service, the D.C. Department of Transportation, in 2006, put up signs indicating the park name as "Meridian Hill Malcolm X Park," because "the community requested the sign include both names on the panel." By the 1960s, the park had become a gathering place for Black activists, and after Malcom X's assassination, a 1970 congressional measure to rename the park for Malcolm X failed, but the name stuck.

7

JOHN R. MORRIS

WESTOVER RYE

*T*here is scant evidence available regarding the whiskey brands John R. Morris sold. He did, however, play a tangential role in the fight against the growing power of the temperance movement in the years before the District went dry. The earliest record found was in an April 1907 industrial and financial newspaper called the *Manufacturers' Record*; it reported, "John R. Morris, 1610 U Street, will erect four two-story brick dwellings and one two-story brick stable on U Street, near 17th Street N.W., to cost about $11,000."

The location of his retail liquor store at 1610 U Street Northwest is primarily confirmed by two murals that were left behind at the site. One was for Morris's "Westover Rye," and the other was for a "Brookville Rye." The murals were done by employees at Stetson's Famous Bar and Grill, which occupied the site from the early 1980s until 2015. Apparently, they discovered several of the old bottles in the basement. The current occupants of the building—the owners of Exiles Bar—have restored the murals, and they are proudly displayed in the open-air back area of the building.

Perhaps the Brookville Rye was a nod to the town in Maryland that was made famous by President James Madison, who stayed there for one day (August 26, 1814) in his attempt to stay ahead of the British troops as they sought to capture Washington, D.C. The town still proudly claims the title "U.S. Capital for a Day."

The fragments of one of Morris's Westover Rye bottles was found in the Adams Morgan neighborhood, next to the U Street neighborhood where his

Left: An artist's rendition of a Westover Rye bottle, based on mural located at 1601 U Street Northwest. *From Christina Owens Knapp.*

Right: An artist's rendition of a Brookville Rye bottle, based on mural located at 1601 U Street Northwest. *From Christina Owens Knapp.*

shop was located. This shows that Morris tried to follow the requirements set forth in the 1906 Food and Drug Act. The bottle identifies the contents as "a blend" and also provides that it was "guaranteed under the national Pure Food and Drug Act of June 30, 1906." Interestingly, the name Westover was not trademarked or copyrighted like his Brookville label was. This is probably because there was another "Westover Rye" that was the flagship brand of Richmond, Virginia's Phil G. Kelly, who, in 1905, registered the name "Westover Rye" with the federal trademark office.

Morris filed an application with the Excise Board on July 9, 1914, to transfer a liquor license from 2025 Virginia Avenue Northwest to 911 Twenty-First Street Northwest. That application was rejected on August 7, 1914. He next appears in the newspaper in December 1914, this time seeking a wholesale liquor license at 2118 Pennsylvania Avenue Northwest

A photograph of the remnants of a Westover Rye bottle found in an Adams Morgan residence. *Courtesy of Scott Cartwright.*

before the Excise Board. At this hearing, Morris was represented by attorney Alexander H. Bell. Under the headline "Lawyers Quarrel at Hearing," it was reported that Bell went after A.E. Shoemaker, the lawyer for the Anti-Saloon League, saying:

> *Who are you and what right have you to appear at a hearing before this Excise Board? The law certainly does not provide for the appearance here of persons with utopian dreams of the elimination of all saloons.*

The December 5, 1914 *Washington Herald* article went on to state:

> *Bell said the men he represented will seek enactment of a law at the coming session of Congress so framed that Shoemaker cannot appear before the board unless he can show he is the authorized attorney of property holders in the neighborhood of the site of the proposed saloon for which a saloon is requested. "You'll have a sweet time getting that law," replied Shoemaker.*

The Excise Board granted Morris's wholesale license on December 10, 1914, but Shoemaker and the Anti-Saloon League were not done with the fight. In March 1915, appearing before a Senate committee looking into how the Excise Board was operating under a recently passed law (1913), Shoemaker argued that over one hundred liquor establishments, including Morris's retail shop at 1610 U Street Northwest, had been illegally licensed, in that they were granted in violation of law—in Morris's particular case, because his shop was being operated on a nonbusiness block or in a residential section of the city.

In a statement to the Excise Board, Shoemaker said:

> *When the board, in 1913, adopted its rules and regulations, the league promptly took exception to several provisions therein as being contrary to the letter as well as the spirit of the law and urged that they be modified. You refused, and the rules and regulations were promulgated as originally adopted. Under and by virtue of them, you have issued licenses that have not the warrant of law. Hotels and clubs located on nonbusiness blocks or in residential sections have barroom licenses. Wholesale liquor establishments are doing business in nonbusiness blocks and residential sections. Hotels with less than fifty bedrooms are enjoying barroom privileges.*
>
> *Prior to the hearings given on the applications for renewal of licenses for the current license year, there was submitted to you by the league for*

your guidance certain reliable information as to more than a hundred of them showing that the places for which licenses were sought were in prohibited localities.

In most instances, for reasons best known to the board, you ignored these legal contentions and attempted to renew many licenses at prohibited places.

By 1915, the Anti-Saloon League, not satisfied with how the new Excise Board was wielding its powers under the law, had used its growing and then considerable political clout to get the Senate to conduct a hearing and gather evidence on the conduct of the board. The Senate, on March 4, 1915, issued the "Report of the Special Committee to Investigate the Conduct of the Excise Board of the District of Columbia." The committee, chaired by Senator Morris Sheppard, detailed a number of complaints (some of them seemingly minor) put forth by Anti-Saloon League lawyers, finding that "the Excise Board, in administering the excise law, has adopted certain rules which, in many instances, change the substance of and letter of the law."

The following are two examples:

1. Three hundred feet from the baneful influence of a saloon.

The excise law provided:

No saloon or other place where intoxicating liquor is sold at retail shall be licensed, allowed or maintained within 300 feet of any alleyway occupied for residence or of places commonly called slums, except upon the unanimous vote of all three members of said Excise Board.

The committee stated:

The plain purpose of this provision was to remove barrooms a reasonable distance at least from these places to protect to that extent the poor people living in them from the baneful influences of saloons.

The League provided to the committee a list of twenty-eight saloons that it asserted were within three hundred feet of inhabited alleys. One of those twenty-eight saloons was owned by "Patrick J. Neligan at 1908 Fourteenth Street Northwest."

The committee continued:

The board has apparently disregarded this purpose. It has granted licenses in practically every instance where applied for within 300 feet of places, and there are three or four or more barrooms located within 300 feet of a single alley.

2. Hotels and saloons of questionable character.

The excise law provided that no license shall be granted to any hotel the character of which, or the character of the proprietor or manager, is shown to board to be objectionable. The Anti-Saloon League provided the committee with two instances—the Grand Hotel (Twenty-Fourth and M Streets) and the Philadelphia House on Pennsylvania Avenue.

The Grand Hotel was granted a license, despite the facts that the proprietor, Edward L. Gardiner, had been previously convicted of dispensing liquor to a minor girl and that a police report, dated October 1914, had been put into evidence at the board hearing on his license:

The manager, Edward L. Gardiner, conducts a garden in the basement of this hotel, where they have music and singing. Dancing is allowed on a platform set aside for that purpose. This is a resort for street walkers and women of questionable character, and the result is a meeting place for men and women. In my opinion, these conditions are objectionable, in connection with a bar, and should be eliminated.

With respect to the Philadelphia House, the committee found, after taking testimony, that its license had been granted, despite it being shown "to be a most disgraceful and disreputable resort for colored prostitutes and for men and women of questionable character."

After presenting almost one thousand pages of testimony and exhibits, Senator Sheppard concluded:

The committee finds no evidence of corruption or venality on the part of the members of the board and believes that each member should be exonerated from any charge or imputation of this character. The committee believes, however, that a careful and dispassionate review of the evidence before us as to the conduct of the board in the administration of the excise law shows that it has nullified its most beneficial features; and that it has encouraged and approved plain evasions and perversions of the law. It is the judgment of the committee that the board has resolved practically every doubt as to law or fact in the interest of the saloons. It has shown no proper comprehension of its duties in the execution of a law framed in the interest of morality and good government. The policy of the board in fostering the liquor traffic to the fullest extent permitted by law and, in many instances, at the expense of both its spirit and its letter is fraught with increasing danger to the health, peace and morals of the people of the District of Columbia.

In any event, all alcohol-related establishments were outlawed in Washington, D.C., just a few years later.

8

JAMES CHARLES McGUIRE

FEDERAL SEAL RYE WHISKEY

James Charles McGuire was one of the liquor merchants who made the Mount Pleasant neighborhood his home. Born in Washington, D.C., in 1875, he graduated from Georgetown University in 1896. By late 1903, he had formed a partnership with John F. Monaghan and opened a liquor store named Monaghan and McGuire at 621 Seventh Street Northwest. Their flagship brand was Federal Seal Rye. The partnership was very short-lived, and by the time the advertisements on the next page ran in June 1904, Monaghan had already left the partnership.

Once McGuire and Monaghan's wholesale supplier, Rosskam, Gerstley and Company, saw how successful their store was, the wholesaler wanted a larger share of the profit. Gertstley induced Monaghan to withdraw from the partnership, and Monaghan became an employee of Rosskam, Gerstley and Company. In executing his plan, Gerstley also claimed that the former partnership owed him a $5,000 payment on a bond the partnership used to secure the purchase of alcohol. When the case went to court in the Supreme Court of the District of Columbia on December 10, 1904, a judgment by confession was obtained against Monaghan. He admitted that the debt was due to the wholesaler. McGuire appealed the decision, first to the Court of Appeals for the District of Columbia, where he again lost, and finally, to the Supreme Court of the United States. The case, *McGuire v. Gerstley*, 204 U.S. 489, was decided on February 25, 1907. Associate Justice Rufus Peckham, writing for the court, affirmed the decision of the court of appeals, making McGuire a three-time loser in the judicial branch.

Top: A Monaghan and McGuire advertisement from the June 17, 1904 *Washington Times*, reproduced here. *Library of Congress.*

Bottom: A Monaghan and McGuire advertisement from the June 11, 1904 *Washington Times*, reproduced here. *Library of Congress.*

Despite this rough start, McGuire went on to become a successful liquor merchant, his store located at 519 Ninth Street Northwest. An advertisement from the December 24, 1905 *Washington Post* shows that McGuire was the "sole distributor" of Federal Seal Rye and that "Uncle Sam Inspects Every Barrel and Guarantees Its Purity." The advertisement also stated that the bottles came "Direct from DISTILLERY to YOU. Straight Rye, 7 years old. One Dollar Per Full Quart." This advertisement indicates that, at least in 1905, Federal Seal Rye was claimed to be a straight whiskey that was bottled-in-bond. In 1913, McGuire was the secretary for the Retail Liquor Dealers' Association (the same organization headed by William Barry of Mount Pleasant Club Whiskey). In 1914, he was appointed teller for the Washington, D.C. Chamber of Commerce.

"BIG TRAIN" JOHNSON'S CUP

An avid Washington Nationals fan, McGuire led a prominent booster club of twenty-eight individuals, who, from time to time, would collect, pool and present money to show fan appreciation for certain team members. One such special occasion was mentioned in the July 24, 1913 *Washington Times* under the headline "Order Is Placed for Johnson Cup—Anniversary Gift from Capital Fans Will Stand Forty Inches High, and Is a Magnificent Piece of Work—Now Up to the Fans to Fill Trophy to Brim with Money." McGuire's booster club was listed along with eight other clubs that raised a total of $605.97, which was presented to ace pitcher Walter Perry "the Big Train" Johnson on August 2, 1913, to mark his six-year anniversary with the Nationals.

Johnson started with the Nationals in 1907 and spent his entire career with the team. He was by far the greatest player to ever wear a uniform for a baseball team in Washington. He was one of the original five players inducted into the National Baseball Hall of Fame when it opened its doors in 1936. Considered one of the most dominant pitchers of all time, Johnson

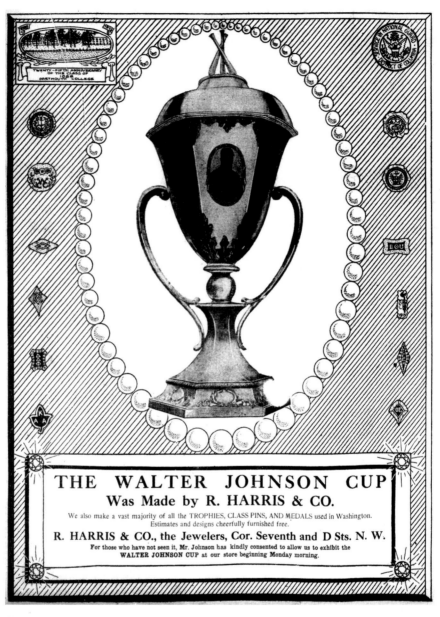

THE WALTER JOHNSON CUP
Was Made by R. HARRIS & CO.

We also make a vast majority of all the TROPHIES, CLASS PINS, AND MEDALS used in Washington.
Estimates and designs cheerfully furnished free.

R. HARRIS & CO., the Jewelers, Cor. Seventh and D Sts. N. W.

For those who have not seen it, Mr. Johnson has kindly consented to allow us to exhibit the
WALTER JOHNSON CUP at our store beginning Monday morning.

Opposite: An artist's rendition of a Federal Seal Whiskey bottle. *From Christina Owens Knapp*.

Above: The Walter Johnson Cup from the August 2, 1913 *Washington Times*, reproduced here. *Library of Congress*.

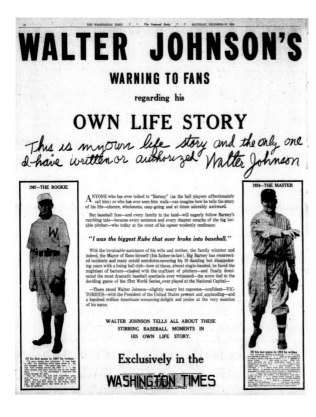

Walter Johnson (the Rookie) from the December 27, 1924 *Washington Times*, reproduced here. *Library of Congress.*

won the pitching Triple Crown (wins, strikeouts and earned run average) three times, in 1913, 1918 and 1924. He was also named the American League's Most Valuable Player twice, in 1913 and 1924. Johnson ended up living only a few blocks away from McGuire in the Mount Pleasant neighborhood, first at the Kenesaw Apartment House at the corner of Sixteenth and Irving (formerly Kenesaw) Streets in 1915 and then at 1843 Irving Street until 1925. When flush with the money he had earned from taking the Nationals to the 1924 World Series, he bought a house on Old Georgetown Road in Bethesda, Maryland.

After Prohibition came to Washington, D.C., in 1917, McGuire closed his liquor store and played an active role in the Al Smith Club of Washington, D.C. Al Smith was a four-time governor of New York, who, in 1923, signed legislation repealing the state's Prohibition statute, leaving its enforcement to the federal government. Smith became the Democratic candidate for president of the United States in 1928. In February 1928, McGuire was appointed as a member on a three-person committee to find a permanent headquarters for the campaign. In June 1928, he was listed as a candidate

A photograph of a Federal Seal Whiskey bottle found in Mount Pleasant. *Courtesy of Greg Lavallee; from Jason Hamacher.*

for the central committee in the Democratic primary for Washington, D.C. A question on the ballot read, "Do you favor national representation for the people of the District of Columbia in the Congress of the United States and in the electoral college?" It seems things in Washington, D.C. politics never change. Smith, a Catholic, went on to lose the election soundly to Herbert Hoover, in part because the temperance movement made a lot of noise about his religion, claiming that the pope would be giving Smith orders.

McGuire died at his home at 3204 Nineteenth Street Northwest in Mount Pleasant on August 31, 1938, and was given a requiem mass at Shrine of the Sacred Heart Church in the neighborhood. He was buried at the Mount Olivet Cemetery. One of McGuire's bottles was found sealed in a wall across the street from where he lived. Interestingly, the label provides that the contents of the bottle was a "blend," which indicates McGuire either switched sources for his whiskey, leaving behind the claim of it being aged seven years and a straight whiskey, or he just relabeled the existing whiskey truthfully to comply with the Pure Food and Drug Act of 1906.

9

CHARLES KRAEMER

FINEZA RYE

The house located at 1841 Park Road Northwest was built in 1906 and is known as the Charles Kraemer House. It is listed as "the finest of several Colonial Revival houses built in the Mount Pleasant area in the early twentieth century" in the Library of Congress's Historical American Building Survey. Kraemer's house is also significant for the role it played in the desegregation of the neighborhood in 1950, when his daughter sold the house to a Black family, a direct affront to the Mount Pleasant Citizens Association. Kraemer built the mansion using the money he made as a liquor merchant between the early 1880s and 1914.

Kraemer emigrated from Germany at the age of twelve, arriving in Washington in 1866. He worked various retail jobs, including running a shop with his fellow German immigrant William Muehleisen, before opening his own store, Chas. Kraemer Wholesale and Retail Wines and Liquors, in 1885, first at 737 Seventh Street Northwest before moving next door to 735 Seventh Street in the early 1890s. He carried many brands and was Washington's wholesale agent for Canadian Club and OFC Rye. He was also the sole distributor of a Tennessee whiskey called Cascade, as a 1904 *Washington Post* article announced:

> It is an acknowledged fact that there is no purer whisky distilled in America than which comes from Tennessee, and "Cascade" is the leader of these Tennessee whiskies. It is entirely free from any deleterious substance and

A photograph of the Charles Kraemer House at 1841 Park Road Northwest in Mount Pleasant. *Library of Congress.*

is purified by filtration through the highest grade of charcoal, which is produced from sugar maple wood. "Cascade" can be found in all leading restaurants and cafés and is distributed in Washington by Mr. Charles Kraemer, 735 Seventh Street.

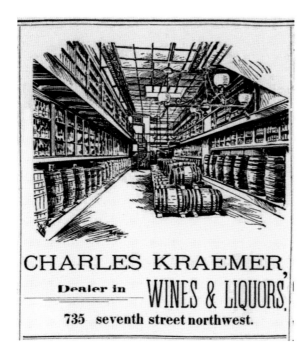

CHARLES KRAEMER,
Dealer in WINES & LIQUORS,
735 seventh street northwest.

A Kraemer advertisement from the September 18, 1897 *Washington Bee*, reproduced here. *Library of Congress.*

Almost from the beginning, Kraemer featured his own brand of rye called Fineza. Between 1895 and 1914, there were at least 270 Fineza advertisements in the *Evening Star* alone. Like most other Washington producers, Kraemer made claims that his Fineza was "pure," and he also touted its medicinal properties, with such claims as, "Kraemer's Fineza Promotes Strength," and "quality made and maintains Fineza Whisky as the preferred stimulant for medicinal use. Smooth, satisfying taste, exquisite bouquet." The mentions of Kraemer (aside from those in his advertisements) are few and far between. From an October 3, 1897 *Washington Post* article, we learn that Kraemer went on a monthlong

> *extended business and pleasure trip combined. He went from here direct to Denver, thence to the famous Manitou Mineral Springs at the base of Pike's Peak, where he will be afforded an opportunity to witness the bottling of this sparkling table water for which he is the sole agent.*

From a July 9, 1898 article, we know that Mrs. Charles Kraemer "has gone to Oakland for the summer." On April 24, 1910, the *Evening Star* reported, "A Peerless touring car has been delivered to Charles Kraemer, finished in Brewster green. It is a four-cylinder forty-horsepower car with a seating capacity

Above, left: A Kraemer advertisement from the July 23, 1904 *Washington Evening Star*, reproduced here. *Library of Congress.*

Above, right: A Kraemer advertisement from the June 18, 1904 *Washington Evening Star*, reproduced here. *Library of Congress.*

Left: A Kraemer advertisement from the January 24, 1904 *Washington Herald*, reproduced here. *Library of Congress.*

A photograph of Kraemer's metal match holder gift. *Jason Hamacher.*

of seven passengers." The car's list price at the time of Kraemer's purchase was the princely sum of $4,300. Known as one of the "Three Ps"—Peerless, Packard and Pierce-Arrow—Peerless was based in Cleveland and operated between 1900 and 1931; it was famous for building luxury cars for the wealthy. The company went bankrupt in the lead-up to the Depression when its clientele went broke. After Prohibition's repeal, the factory was retooled to produce beer after the company obtained a license to make Carling Black Label and Red Cap ale brands from the Brewing Corporation of Canada.

Keen to separate himself from the competition, Kraemer was known to give away gifts bearing his logo and store location for Fineza. One particularly fine example is a small metal match safe made to look like a whiskey flask. The top opens to reveal a small compartment where one could store wooden matches.

By 1914, it seems that Kraemer wanted to get out of the liquor industry. He first sought to transfer his liquor license to M.S. Frost. The transfer, which was ultimately denied, sought to move Kraemer's license at 733 Seventh Street to Frost's location at 831 Seventh Street. According to a July 25, 1914 *Evening Star* article, protests were made by Hyman Dodek, who owned a women's furnishing store next door to the proposed saloon, and by the Anti-Saloon League. A few weeks later, with a new proposed owner, James O. Vermillion, the transfer was approved by the Excise Board.

In retirement, Kraemer took to growing fruit at his Park Road house. Apparently, he was pretty good at it, as there is an *Evening Star* article, dated November 25, 1928, titled "Washington Man Raises Big Lemon: Fruit Grown at Park Road Residence Almost as Big as Cantaloupe." In the article, Kraemer acknowledged that in growing the pound-and-a-half lemon, he adhered to the Department of Agriculture's bulletins on fruit culture. The article concluded:

> *On a 100-by-125-foot lot in the rear of his residence, Kraemer applies intensified methods of culture on a number of fruits, with the apple leading in annual yield. Two of his best trees produced a total of twenty-eight bushels this year, Kraemer said.*

THE DRIVE TO KEEP MOUNT PLEASANT WHITE: THE MOUNT PLEASANT CITIZENS' ASSOCIATION

Upon Kraemer's death in 1932 at the age of seventy-two, the house at 1841 Park Road went to his daughter, Lillian Curry. Attached to the house was a racial restrictive covenant that Kraemer, as was the case with about 90 percent of the Mount Pleasant residents of the time, had signed. The goal of such covenants (and the Mount Pleasant Citizens' Association, or MPCA, which promoted them) was to restrict Black Americans from living in particular areas of the city, to include Mount Pleasant.

A May 23, 1923 *Evening Star* article provides a glimpse into the MPCA, which was founded in 1910 with ten initial members. By 1923, there were over six hundred active members. The MPCA was originally formed with the purpose of buying the land at the end of the Mount Pleasant car line that would then be used to build a "beauty spot" for a park. This area is now known as Lamont Park, and it is where the weekly farmers' market takes place. The park was developed and owned by the MPCA until the city took it over years later. According to the article, the MPCA played key roles in obtaining the land for both the public library and Bancroft Elementary School. The article identified the then-current officers as Major Robert Young of 1626 Newton Street, president, and Hugh C. Russell of 3349 Eighteenth Street, vice-president.

The MPCA took a number of steps to attempt to maintain the racial and economic status quo as Washington changed around them. The following is an excerpt from the 1929 MPCA "agreement" that implemented the covenant for the fifty-plus residences that lined the north and south sides of Nineteenth Street, where the original Mount Pleasant Club Whiskey bottle was found. Interestingly, one of the signatories of the document was Blanche McGuire, the wife of J. Charles McGuire, who lived at 3204 Nineteenth Street.

Now, therefore, in consideration of the premises and the sum of one dollar ($1.00) each to the other in hand paid, the parties do hereby mutually covenant, promise and agree each with the other and for their respective heirs and assigns, that no part of the land now owned by the parties hereto, a more detailed description of said property being given after the respective signatures hereto, shall ever be used or occupied by, or sold, conveyed, leased, rented or given, to negros or any person or persons of the negro race or blood. This covenant shall run with the land and bind the respective heirs and *assigns of the parties hereto for a period of fifty (50) years from and after the date of these presents.*

By the early 1920s, faced with both (1) the construction and subsequent widening of Sixteenth Street that effectively split the neighborhood and (2) what the MPCA saw as the inevitable invasion of Black Americans as they began to move into parts of the city to the south and east of Mount Pleasant, the MPCA made the decision to abandon the part of the neighborhood between Fourteenth and Sixteenth Streets and to move the eastern boundary of the neighborhood to Sixteenth Street, ceding the historical commercial center of the neighborhood to Columbia Heights.

A 1948 report titled "Segregation in Washington, a Report of the National Committee on Segregation in the Nation's Capitol" included text from another Kenesaw Mountain Landis, who shared the same name with his uncle the federal judge who became the commissioner of Major League Baseball who dealt with the White Sox scandal after producing one of the opinions favorable to Dr. Wiley's cause during the war to define whiskey.

The 1948 report stated:

Segregation is Good Business

The local real estate board has nothing against Negroes as homeowners. But "exclusiveness" has a market value and is a substantial factor in determining what many white people will offer for residential properties. Thus, segregation is good business.

By throwing up racial barriers, a realtor can capitalize on the racial feelings of some of his customers without making the property less valuable to others. Once this process starts, racial prejudice becomes an investment and enters into the resale price of all lots in the area.

The report, in discussing the role of citizens' associations, provides:

Originally, the citizens' associations were neighborhood improvement societies, interested in such things as trees and flowers, schools, parks and improved city services. Not until the 1920s did they become actively concerned in the containment of Negroes and turn into the front line for the real estate interest.

In the drive to exclude to exclude the Negro, the federated citizens' associations have functioned as the front-line shock troops, completing his encirclement by a network of mutual defense pacts or agreements not to sell erected all around the inner zones of the city. Their job has been to hold the line and sound the alarm whenever "danger" threatens.

This is exactly the role the Mount Pleasant Citizens' Association played.

One of the earliest recorded deeds with a racially restrictive covenant in the neighborhood (Ingleside) was filed on March 23, 1911, between the Middaugh and Shannon Corporation and Jane Davis Bradford. In part, it reads:

Said lot shall never be rented, leased, sold or transferred or conveyed to or in trust for any negro or colored person under penalty of $2,000, which shall be a lien against said property.

The use of racially restrictive covenants took off in 1917, when the Supreme Court ruled in the case *Buchanan v. Warley*, saying that state-sponsored segregation ordinances violated the Fourteenth Amendment. Segregationist citizens' associations like MPCA turned to implementing racially restrictive covenants in 1927, one year after the Supreme Court upheld the use of racially restrictive covenants in its 1926 ruling in *Corrigan v. Buckley*, finding that, unlike the race-based legislation that was forced on residents by the government, individuals entering into covenant agreements were doing so of their own volition and were thus beyond the reach of the court.

The MPCA hired a representative who went door to door in the neighborhood to obtain signatures. If the property owner refused to sign, they were paid a follow-up visit by members of the Restrictive Covenants Committee. The MPCA even performed all the required administrative legwork—they had someone draft the documents, get them notarized, pay the $1.50 filing fee and file them with the recorder of deeds. The MPCA even had a clerk at the city assessor's office who would let the MPCA know whenever a property in the neighborhood changed hands. The MPCA also paid close attention to the properties that went into foreclosure, as this was one of the ways the covenant could become invalid.

In the 1937 case *Grady v. Garland*, the Supreme Court declined to review a D.C. Court of Appeals case that upheld a racially restrictive covenant in which white owners wanted to terminate the thirty-year restriction so that they could sell to whomever they wanted in the increasingly Black neighborhood of Eckington. In upholding the covenant, the court stated that covenants created "a barrier against the eastward movement of the colored population into restricted areas." The president of the Federation of Citizens' Associations was quoted in the October 15, 1947 *Washington Post* as saying, "Race segregation here [in Washington, D.C.,] is a natural state, and certain groups which agitate against it are unscrupulous and un-American."

In May 1948, the Supreme Court finally put an end to the government's enforcement of racially restrictive covenants in the decision *Shelley v. Kraemer*. Nope, this was a different Kraemer—Louis D. Kraemer was from St. Louis, and he sued his neighbor who had the audacity to sell his property to a Black American, despite the racially restrictive covenant attached to it. In the decision, the court did not outlaw the covenants—that didn't happen until 1968 with the passage of the 1968 Fair Housing Act, but it did end the government's enforcement of such covenants. In response to this change of affairs, the MPCA sought to exploit a loophole left by the case by giving out voluntary contracts to residents to sign that stated they would not sell their properties to "anyone not of the Caucasian race." The following is a sample agreement that was prepared by the Mount Pleasant Citizens' Association in October 1948:

> *Whereas it is deemed necessary to continue in the spirit of such covenants for the protection of the value of our properties and the character of the community and to preserve what we believe to be our inherent right and prerogative.*
>
> *We, the undersigned owners of real estate in the Mount Pleasant area of the District of Columbia identified opposite our names in consideration of the mutual agreement of other property owners in the Mount Pleasant area, hereby agree that we will not sell, transfer or lease such properties or any part thereof to any person or persons other than those of the Caucasian race.*
>
> *We further agree to furnish the Mount Pleasant Citizens' Association promptly with all information we may receive of any attempt by any person not of the Caucasian race to purchase, acquire or occupy any such property and to cooperate with said association in the preservation of the integrity of our community in accordance with the tenor of this agreement.*

In 1950, the Mount Pleasant Citizens' Association established a Real Estate Protective Committee and funded it to allow the Mount Pleasant Citizens' Association to obtain options on properties that were potentially going to be sold to Black Americans. The 1948 report summed up the Mount Pleasant Citizens' Association's predicament:

White Victims of Segregation

The white people who belong to these citizens' associations are themselves victims in the overall segregation policy. The profit is not for them. The fact that the Negro's exclusion can be capitalized is their main worry. What they fear is the high price that colored people are forced to pay and are willing to offer. They don't want to sell.

What is important to most whites is the value of the property as a place to live, and this value is threatened by the construction of racial barricades. With each Nego segregated, the fear increases in adjacent white communities, as if a dam were about to break. When a crack appears, panic may ensue, and the white owner may suffer an actual monetary loss.

But worse than any derangement in property value is what happens to relations of men. When bigotry is incorporated, normal human values are destroyed, and every Negro becomes a menace.

With that, the stage was set for Kraemer's daughter, Lillian, to try to sell the house at 1841 Park Road to a Black gynecologist at Howard University named Dr. Robert Deane in 1950. When the members of MPCA found out about the transaction, they were outraged—going so far as to trying to sue Lillian to stop the sale based on the old covenant. They lost, and Mount Pleasant got its first Black family.

10

PATRICK J. DRURY

HAVILAND RYE WHISKEY

*A*side from this nicely preserved bottle (found in a house in the Mount Pleasant neighborhood of Washington, D.C.), not much could be found regarding Patrick J. Drury and his involvement in the liquor trade. Much more can be found from his older brother Peter A. Drury and his involvement as the vice-president and treasurer of the Abner-Drury Brewery of the in the District (he was maybe the only Irishman in the German-heavy brewing trade in the city). Born on January 4, 1867, in Castlereagh, Roscommon County, Ireland, Drury immigrated to the United States in 1887 and became a naturalized citizen on July 21, 1893. He lived at 1422 Harvard Street Northwest. He was granted his first liquor license for a store at 1228 D Street Northwest on December 5, 1898. The P.J. Drury Co. was incorporated in the District on December 1, 1904. Eventually, he moved to 210 Tenth Street Northwest. It is obvious that the bottle illustrated in this book was produced sometime after the passage of the 1906 Food and Drug Act. It seems that Drury took quite literally the dictate of section 9 of the act, which provided for the inclusion that a dealer would not be prosecuted if a guarantee was provided on a liquor bottle that the contents of the bottle were not adulterated or misbranded.

In both 1906 and 1907, Drury was involved in wagon accidents that made their way into the local newspapers. In the first, dated January 4, 1906, under the headline "Exciting Runaway—Mrs. F.E. Zepp Severely Injured and Her Horse Killed," it was reported that Mrs. Zepp of

Left: A photograph of a P.J. Drury Co.'s Haviland Rye bottle found in Mount Pleasant. *Courtesy of Deirdre Warner-Kramer; from Jason Hamacher.*

Below: Patrick J. Drury's passport photograph (1923). *National Archives and Records Administration.*

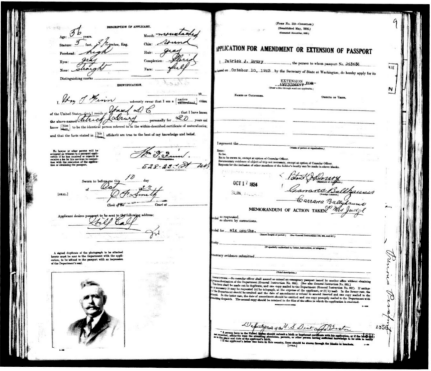

Arlington, Virginia, lost control of her wagon when her horse became frightened and bolted around H Street. With her carriage overturned and her son thrown out but unharmed:

> *Mrs. Zepp was dragged some distance and injured about the shoulder. The animal continued as far as Seventh and G Streets, where a collision occurred between the runaway team and a horse and carriage owned by P.J. Drury of 210 Tenth Street Northwest, the shaft of the latter vehicle fatally wounding the horse, Mrs. Zepp was taken to the Emergency Hospital for treatment.*

With another accident reported in the July 13, 1907 edition of the *Washington Times*, Drury was sued for $5,000 for damages in relation to a wagon accident that took place on May 14, 1907. It was alleged that, at the intersection of Fourteenth Street and Rhode Island Avenue, Drury ran over the complainant, Charles Claveloux, with his wagon, leaving Claveloux severely injured.

In the November 17, 1911 *Washington Times* article, the result of a lawsuit was reported, and it involved Drury's company, the P.J. Drury Company. The suit was filed against a former longtime employee named James W. Cumming. The company was awarded $1,320. In 1913, the company brought another civil suit against a Frank J. Powers, seeking $1,300. The Excise Board, in 1914, granted Drury's transfer application from 210 Tenth Street to 327 Thirteenth Street Northwest.

Things must not have gone well for Drury, as in the May 28, 1916 edition of the *Evening Star*, it was reported that he had been arrested for passing a bad check. "It was charged that he passed a worthless check on Frank Altemus. Bond in the sum of $1.00 was furnished for his appearance in police court, and he was detained at police headquarters only a few minutes." Drury died on February 25, 1949, and was provided a requiem mass at the Shrine of the Sacred Heart Catholic Church at Sixteenth Street and Park Road Northwest. He was then buried in Mount Olivet Cemetery.

An artist's rendition of a Haviland Rye bottle. *Christina Owens Knapp.*

11

CHRISTIAN XANDER

OLD RESERVE RYE

.

Christian Xander was the leader of a liquor empire that included his brothers Karl and Jacob and even his son Henry. He first appeared on his own in the March 7, 1870 edition of the *Evening Star*:

> *The attention of our readers is respectfully called to the advertisement of Mr. Christian Xander of the late firm of Xander and Muehleisen, which can be found in our columns. Mr. Xander has taken the spacious store No. 913 Seventh Street, between I Street and Massachusetts Avenue, where he has a large stock of imported and domestic liquors of the best brands.*

According to his May 8, 1908 obituary, Xander died of rheumatism. He had gone to Hot Springs, Arkansas, the previous year in the hopes that the waters would help his ailment. However, upon his return, he told relatives and friends that he had not been helped by the waters and expressed the opinion he would never recover. Xander was born in 1837 in the town of Großweier, Baden-Württemberg, Germany (the same region as his friend Muehleisen). He attended school until the age of fourteen, when he was forced to go to work to provide for his mother and his siblings after his father died. He saved money, and at the age of sixteen, in 1853, he immigrated to New York City, where he worked at a bakery in a hotel. From his obituary:

> *In 1859, there were few wine houses of consequence in the national capital. The fact that the city was the home of highest officials in government life,*

LAST RITES SUNDAY

Funeral Services Over Remains of Christian Xauder.

UNION VETERAN AND MASON

Among Most Prominent German-American Citizens in District.

WAS VICTIM OF RHEUMATISM

Member of Maennerchor Society, the Arion Society and Connected With Business Interests.

Funeral services over the remains of Christian Xander will be held at 2 o'clock Sunday afternoon at the Xander home, 909 7th street. The officiating clergyman will be Rev. Paul A. Mentzel, pastor of the Concordia Lutheran Church and a personal friend of Mr. Xander, who had been for years a leading member of the congregation. The interment will be in Prospect Hill cemetery.

The death of Christian Xander occurred at 7:30 o'clock last evening, and resulted from rheumatism, from which disease he had been a sufferer for about twenty-five years. He went to Hot Springs in August last. When he returned he told relatives and friends he had not been

Above: An artist's rendition of a Xander's Old Reserve bottle. *Christina Owens Knapp.*

Right: Christian Xander's obituary excerpt from the May 8, 1908 *Washington Evening Star*, reproduced here. *Library of Congress.*

Christian Xander.

helped by the waters, and expressed the opinion he would never recover. Since his return to Washington he has had a number of attacks which confined him to the bed.

Mr. Xander became ill three weeks ago and gradually grew worse. For a week before his death he was unconscious and subject to delirium. During the past few days he was unable to move.

Dr. G. K. G. Baier was in constant attendance, and two other physicians, Dr. G. N. Acker and Dr. S. S. Adams, were called in for consultation.

When the end came there were present around the bedside his son, Henry Xander; his daughter, Mrs. Minnie Iseman; his sister-in-law, Mrs. Jacob Xander, and his grandson, George Xander.

Prominent Citizen.

as well as many wealthy foreigners, struck Mr. Xander. After surveying the field, he decided this city was in need of a first-class wine house to supply the tables of the rich. He established that year the business in which he engaged until his death, except for a short period during the Civil War.

Xander served in the Union army during the Civil War. Noted as "one of the most prominent German American citizens of the District," he was connected to the Sangerbund, a chorus that is still active today and dedicated to the study and performance of German classical and folk repertoire. He was also the treasurer of the Washington Schuetzen Verein organization for eighteen years. Xander was also a baseball enthusiast who expressed regret when he could no longer support the Washington teams in person at the games.

The first image on the following page shows Xander in front of his offices and retail store, which he built in 1885. The second shows Xander's vaults and warehouses, built at 630 Massachusetts Avenue, which were connected to his store in the rear. The following is a description of Xander's business from the 1884 *Washington and Its Points of Interest Illustrated*:

To gain public confidence is one of the first and most essential steps that a businessman can take when he embarks in any line of trade, and when once the pace is set and the quality and genuineness of his wares established, he may safely feel that he is on the high road to success. This has been the rule by which Mr. Chr. Xander has worked since embarking in business over a quarter-century ago. He is one of the most reliable and oldest importers and wholesale dealers in fine wines and liquors in Washington and has a finely fitted place of business at 909 Seventh Street Northwest. Born in Germany, Mr. Xander came out to the States forty-one years ago, and his commercial career has been one of prosperity. He has an eligibly located place, the building being built expressly for his business. He occupies three floors, 25-by-150 feet in space, with a warehouse two stories in height, 30-by-129 feet, a 10-foot-high vault running the length from the winery in the rear to Massachusetts Avenue. His wholesale trade, calculated mainly to be local, has, in a natural way, expanded throughout the surrounding eight states without any soliciting agents. His employees in warehouses, cellars and sale store number seven, two of these drivers. His stock of the rarest and exceptionally old whiskies is well known as one of the richest in the Union. Special brands are Chr. Xander's "Old Private Stock," "Old Stock," "Old Reserve," "Family Brand" and "Gold Medal." His medicinal proprietary

Left: A photograph of Christin Xander in front of his retail store at 909 Seventh Street Northwest. *Library of Congress.*

Right: A photograph of Christian Xander in front of his Vaults and Warehouse at 630 Massachusetts Avenue Northwest. *Library of Congress.*

beverages are: Melliston, wild cherry cordial, blackberry cordials, stomach bitters, cocoa wine. From his winery: all-grape Virginia port and Ives and Norton's Virginia clarets. He handles all the leading high grades of liquors, wines, etc. He has a large stock of goods in bond and free and handles these for his customers in case lots or bulk. Such is Mr. Xander's reputation in this country throughout the trade that his name on parcels is a sufficient guarantee of their high quality and absolute purity and maturity. His premises and vaults were built with the view to perfect depuration and maturing of wines and liquors, and his goods, sold direct and by retailers, are the accepted standards in hotels and private families. Mr. Xander's business policy is one of unwavering integrity, and his house stands in the first rank of reliable commercial firms.

A Christian Xander advertisement for ready-to-drink cocktails, featuring his Old Reserve Whiskey, from the January 31, 1904 *Washington Times*, reproduced here. *Library of Congress.*

This advertisement from the January 31, 1904 edition of the *Washington Times* shows that Xander was an innovator who may have been one of the first to sell what today are known as ready-to-drink cocktails, which have recently taken off in popularity.

JACOB XANDER

Christian's brothers Jacob and Karl were also important players in the Washington, D.C. liquor scene and had their own write-ups in the 1894 *Points of Interest* book:

> *Jacob Xander, wines and liquors, 1315 Seventh Street Northwest, between N and O Streets. This house was established by the present proprietor about*

Jacob Xander,

DEALER IN

Wines and Liquors,

1315 Seventh Street, N. W.

Between N and O Streets

A Jacob Xander advertisement from the January 8, 1897 *Washington Bee*, reproduced here. *Library of Congress.*

eighteen years ago and has steadily grown in prestige and popularity. The store is twenty-two by ninety feet in area and fitted up with every accessory necessary in the trade. The finest line of liquors, brandies, cordials and imported and domestic wines are constantly kept in stock and sold in any quantity, either by the glass pint, quart, gallon or in case lots. Mr. Xander is a native of Germany and an expert in all kinds of liquors and buys direct and handles only the best standard brands. He has built up a large family trade in all kinds of liquors, and his patrons are always contented. He is a wide-awake, active and reputable businessman and well known in mercantile circles.

KARL XANDER

Karl Xander, liquors, 439 K Street Northwest. This gentleman is a native German and came to the States in 1872. He established his present business in this city in 1885, and in 1889, he embarked in the wholesale trade and has built up a large and prosperous patronage. Mr. Xander occupies a handsome building, twenty-two by seventy-five feet in [area]. *It is one of the finest fitted and elaborately appointed places in the city, and every requirement for the successful conduct of a large business is provided. He carries in stock at all times one of the largest and most complete lines of fine wines and liquors to be found in the city. The long experience of Mr. Xander in this line of trade has made him a connoisseur in these goods, and only the most reliable and those known to be strictly pure are handled. He is a direct importer of wines of the finest vintage and handles them both at wholesale and retail and in any quantity to suit the purchaser. Every standard brand of champagne, hock, rhine, claret and other blends of wines is to be found here and is sold at the lowest prices commensurate with the excellent quality. He also makes a specialty of fine whiskies, cordials, gins, brandies and rums and has made a large trade on his "Southern Bouquet" whisky and "Millvale," which are pronounced by expert judges to be the choicest blended and aged liquors in the market. The leading hotels, restaurants and buffets, as well as the choicest family trade, are supplied by*

Mr. Xander. He does a large retail trade, having a handsomely fitted buffet, which is completely stocked with nice goods of every kind. Mr. Xander is one of the most prominent German Americans in the city and stands at the very pinnacle in commercial rectitude and in the esteem of the public. He is a well-known member of several of the leading societies of the city and takes as prominent a position in social circles as he maintains his business. Goods bearing the name Xander carry a guarantee of purity and age and are those that are sought by every connoisseur.

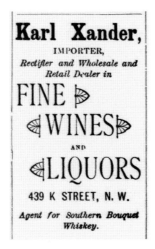

A Karl Xander advertisement from the January 8, 1897 *Washington Bee,* reproduced here. *Library of Congress.*

The Xanders' advertisements often appeared together in the newspapers, as in this October 2, 1897 *Washington Bee* advertisement: "Karl Xander is at 439 K Street Northwest, and Jacob Xander is at 1315 Seventh Street Northwest. These are first-class houses." In August 1899, Karl had an application to erect "a stationary hanging awning frame in front of his premises" denied by the city commissioners because "permanent awning frames have seriously interfered with the work of the fire department on many occasions," and they obstructed the sidewalks.

Karl's daughter Carrie kept her marriage to Thomas Luckett, a telegraph operator at the Shoreham, a secret—at least according to a July 28, 1897 *Evening Star* article titled "Kept Their Secret: Announcement of a June Marriage Just Made by Bride." On June 23, the couple went for a river excursion:

And made a stop at Alexandria, where they were married. After enjoying a sail further down the Potomac, they returned to the city and to their respective homes without taking their friends into their confidence over their important step.

One day last week, the young bride went to Colonial Beach and from that point wrote to her parents, informing them of her marriage. Yesterday, the family joined the couple at the beach to extend congratulations.

HENRY XANDER

Henry Xander was a music teacher with his own studio downtown. He spent part of his youth in Europe learning music, but he also worked during the evenings in his father's store and eventually obtained his own liquor license in 1898 for a store at 3057 K Street Northwest. Henry was also the music director at the Washington Saengerbund for many years and was granted a lifetime membership by the organization upon his retirement from that position. According to a April 18, 1910 *Evening Star* article, "It was explained that Mr. Xander's business engagements were such to compel his resignation." The article continued, "A feature of the evening was Prof. Xander's three compositions on the piano: 'Slumber Song,' 'Springtide' and 'Valse Brillante.'"

In an interesting aside, Henry made the paper again on October 10, 1909, this time because someone had stolen his car. In the *Washington Herald* article titled "Shoe Only Clew: Police Seek Men Who Stole Automobile of Henry Xander," it was reported that Henry's nephew George Eiseman had parked the car at Henry's home at 909 Seventh Street on Friday night, and when he looked for it the next morning, it was gone. The article provided:

> *With the aid of a shoe as a single clew* [sic], *detectives are tracing three men who stole an automobile from Henry Xander, director of the Saengerbund.*
>
> *About 1 o'clock yesterday morning, a touring car containing three men, apparently drunk, sped across the highway bridge. It was found a few hours later at the bottom of a twenty-foot embankment at the end of the bridge. The machine was badly damaged. A no. 8 shoe was found in the bottom of the automobile. Detectives believe the shoe was worn by one of the men who occupied the car and are searching for him.*

Clew is an archaic spelling of *clue* that can be found in many old newspapers. The highway bridge spanned the Potomac River from 1906 to 1969, when it was replaced by the Fourteenth Street Bridge. There is no word on whether the police ever found the man who lost his shoe.

12

WILLIAM MUEHLEISEN SR.

OAKMONT RYE

etween 1867 and 1917, the father-and-son team of William Muehleisen Sr. and William Muehleisen Jr. was a prominent fixture in the Washington, D.C. liquor trade. William Muehleisen Sr. was born on December 1, 1841, in Stadtkreis Stuttgart, Baden-Württemberg, Germany. He immigrated to the United States at the age of eighteen. He died on December 1, 1889. His obituary, published in the December 3, 1889 edition of the *Washington Evening Star*, stated that he died of consumption at the age of forty-eight, right before his children were to present him with a birthday present. He first entered the liquor business with Andrew Sprohs before forming a partnership with Christian Xander. His partnership with Xander lasted only three years, as evidenced by the notice published in the September 23, 1871 edition of the *Evening Star*:

> *Notice to the Public—All bills due the late firm of XANDER and MUEHLEISEN will, from this date, be collected by Wm. Muehleisen only. September 22nd, 1871.*

Muehleisen then struck out on his own at a store located at 918 Fifth Street, between I and K Streets Northwest. He was a leading member of the District's German American citizens. Like his friend Christian Xander, he too acted as the treasurer of the Park of the Washington Schuetzen Verein organization for a time. Opened as the Civil War was winding down, Washington's Schuetzen Park was located where the present-day neighborhood of Park View now stands. This park, like others that popped up in cities across the country during this time, was the German American version of a country club, where marksmanship, rather than golf, was featured. Shooting contests using a specifically designed weapon called a Schuetzen rifle that contained precision sights, double triggers and sculptured cheek pieces were often held. The park was destroyed by a fire in 1879 and rebuilt the following year, but it was permanently closed in 1891. Attempts to build another park after the Park View neighborhood was established on the Schuezten Park's original footprint were quashed by a new law that was passed when a nearby Old Soldier's Home was built. The law forbade the sale of alcohol within a mile of the home.

In an 1887 book titled *Historical Sketches of Our Capital City of Our Country: A Brief Review of Many of Its Leading and Enterprising Business and Professional Men*, it was written of William Senior:

> *Twenty years since the above-named gentleman established himself as an importer and dealer in foreign and domestic wines and liquors at 918 Fifth Street Northwest. The business of this establishment has grown to such an extent within that time that the proprietor has been compelled to build a more commodious house, which is now in course of construction and will be completed with a few days at No. 916 Fifth Street Northwest. This building is a three-story brick, twenty-two-by-ninety feet, with [a] cellar the entire length of the house, finished in the most approved manner as to light and ventilation, the first floor to be occupied as office and salesrooms, the second and third for wareroom purposes. When finished, it will be complete in all appointments and into which will be transferred his large stock of old bourbon and rye whiskies, foreign and domestic wines and mineral waters, including the most popular brands of each. Mr. Muehleisen is a native of Germany, born in 1840, came to the United States in 1855 and engaged in the liquor business in early life. His long experience and practical sense have placed him prominently among the successful businessmen of Washington.*

William Muehleisen Jr.

William Muehleisen Jr. took over his father's business after William Sr. died. The Muehleisens' flagship brand was Oakmont Rye Whiskey. The label was trademarked in 1901. The bottle depicted in this book was produced after the 1906 Pure Food and Drug Act was passed, and as specified in accordance

Left: An artist's rendition of a Muehleisen's Oakmont Rye bottle. *Christina Owens Knapp.*

Right: A William Muehleisen Jr.'s Mount Vernon Savings Bank advertisement from the May 13, 1920 *Washington Times*, reproduced here. *Library of Congress.*

with section 8 of the act, the whiskey is listed as a "blend," meaning that the whiskey was rectified and not a straight whiskey. And in accordance with section 9, the label contains a guarantee. They put an additional caution on the bottle's label that read, "This whiskey is bottled under our personal supervision. The original contents of this package are not adulterated or misbranded. See that seal over the cork is not broken."

After being forced out of the liquor business once the District went dry in 1917, William Jr. reinvented himself as a banker. As one of the founders of the Mount Vernon Savings Bank, he served as its first president until 1928 and remained on its board until it failed in the 1930s. The bank was located at Ninth Street and Mount Vernon Place Northwest in the International Machinists building. William Jr. died on December 17, 1942, and was buried in the family plot in the Prospect Hill Cemetery, where most German Americans in the District were buried.

13

JAMES THARP

BERKELEY PURE RYE

*J*ames Tharp and his sons took an expansive view of the way they advertised their brand, Berkeley Rye. Their advertisements were frequently published in local papers, using creative and unique methods to capture the public's attention, patronage and loyalty. As the "An Honest Whiskey" advertisement suggests, Tharp touted the medicinal values of his Berkeley Rye to treat "consumption weakness, coughs and bronchial troubles." Born in 1829 in Zanesville, Ohio, he fought with the Union army in the Civil War. In the 1870 census, his occupation is listed as "tobacconist"; in the 1800 census, he is listed in the business of "wholesale liquor"; and in the 1900 census, he is referred to as a "liquor dealer." Tharp was known to draft advertisements that incorporated and merged legitimate news stories with inducements to try his brand. An example from the February 2, 1890 *Washington Sunday Critic* provides:

One Way to Settle the Unpleasantness in the H. of R.

There is no occasion for all this filibustering in the House of Representatives for several days past if the proper course was pursued. Why not formulate immediately some feasible rules by which the House can be governed without the friction? In the absence of these much needed rules, it may be in order to pacify the warring factions that they go direct

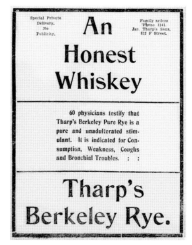 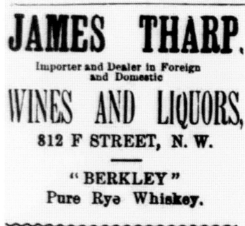

Left: A James Tharp advertisement from the March 17, 1902 *Washington Times*, reproduced here. *Library of Congress.*

Right: A James Tharp advertisement from the January 8, 1897 *Washington Bee*, reproduced here. *Library of Congress.*

> *to Mr. James Tharp's at 818 F Street Northwest, and by the time that all will have indulged in two rounds of that pure old Rye Berkeley Whisky, all difference will be speedily reconciled, and Congressional business will be resumed at the old stand.*

Tharp moved his store three doors down to 812 F Street at the end of 1895. In the January 27, 1896 edition of the *Evening Star*, under the title, "Tharp's Elegantly Fitted-Up New Liquor Establishment," the reason for the move was provided:

> *Mr. Tharp's business has increased to such extensive proportions that his old* [storefront] *was entirely inadequate to accommodate his many patrons of many years' standing, who will not drink any other brand of liquor as a tonic or beverage except his "celebrated Old Rye Berkeley Whisky," which ranks preeminently as the purest and finest tonic in the nation's capital, and as a beverage, it has no equal.*

In another "almost news" advertisement, this one from the March 23, 1898 *Washington Times*, Tharp again proposes his brand as a remedy:

An Ugly Fall

> *A young bicycle rider fell from his wheel in front of 237 B Street Southeast yesterday afternoon and was rendered unconscious. He was removed to his home, No. 1211 Massachusetts Avenue, in the patrol wagon.*
>
> *If someone had only had a flask of Tharp's Pure Berkeley Whisky, he might have been revived at once, and thus obviated the anxiety of his relatives. It is only one dollar for a full quart at Jas. Tharp's, 812 F Street Northwest.*

In another advertisement, dated February 7, 1898, from the *Evening Times*, Tharp touches on contemporary events. The advertisement plays on the relationship between Marcus Alonzo "Mark" Hanna and President William McKinley. Hanna was a wealthy Cleveland, Ohio–based businessman who had used his money and influence to bolster the presidential campaigns of fellow Ohioans Rutherford B. Hayes in 1876 and James Garfield in 1880. Hanna acted as McKinley's campaign manager in 1896. By way of thanks, McKinley had offered Hanna his choice of cabinet positions.

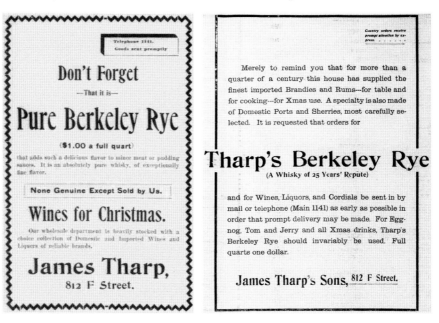

Left: A James Tharp advertisement from the December 11, 1899 *Washington Times*, reproduced here. *Library of Congress.*

Right: A James Tharp advertisement from the December 18, 1901 *Washington Times*, reproduced here. *Library of Congress.*

Mr. McKinley Says So

Mr. McKinley, president of the United States, was much annoyed when it was stated by the New York press that Mr. Hanna, his political sponsor, would have quarters in the White House. Mr. Hanna, it is understood, is still at the Arlington, and when he feels like it, he calls for Berkeley Pure Rye. Sold only by James Tharp, 812 F Street.

Tharp died at the age of seventy-three on February 28, 1901, while in Hot Springs, Arkansas. His son Walter took over running the family business. This is when the Tharp advertisements became even more interesting and amusing.

In addition to the usual Tharp advertisements, Walter began buying large amounts of space in the newspapers to run rhymes about Berkeley Rye set to popular tunes and rhymes. This one is from the September 1, 1901 edition of the *Washington Times:*

The Man from "Quaker Town"
on
"BERKELEY PURE RYE"

A man came from "Quaker Town"
To this city of great renown
Did wander far, and wondered why
He couldn't get some purest rye.
Because he didn't try at Tharp's.
A native of this great big city,
Upon the stranger did take pity.
"In sooth, dear stranger," did he say.
"Just come with me, I'll show you the way—
To Tharp's."
"Pray tarry not, my Quaker friend
Haste thou with me, and we will wend
Our footsteps wither we may buy
'Berkeley Pure Rye'—its magic name
Hath o'erspread Washington with fame
For its excellence."
And thus, this man from "Quaker Town,"
With solemn face—almost a frown
Imbibed a glass or two—meanwhile,

His face o'erspreading with a smile
of appreciation.
"Verily, friend, thou speakest right.
This rye hath merits out of sight,
'Tis mild, 'tis mellow, no connoisseur
Could hesitate at 'Berkeley Pure'
For Quality."
Thus praised the man from "Quaker Town"
This "Berkely Pure" of much renown.
"Methinks," quoth he, "I can't do wrong
In taking home a demijohn
of 'Berkeley Pure Rye."'

MORAL: If you want an absolutely pure rye whisky, a foe to malaria, a tonic and a stimulant, see that you get THARP'S BERKELEY PURE RYE.

The following is a Christmas-themed advertisement from December 14, 1902:

Air: In the Gloaming
THE BACHELOR'S REVERIE

Hark! The merry bells are ringing
In the clear and crispy air,
And old "SANTA CLAUS" is bringing
Presents for the brave and fair.
As a child, I loved KRIS KRINGLE.
As a man, I love him sure,
For I guess his thoughts will mingle
In my share of BERKELEY PURE.
While "Yule" log burns up brightly
(Perchance because we're short of coal)
We will gather round it nightly,
Each communing, soul to soul.
Let each bumper be full flowing
Of the finest we can buy,
To toast our friends, and health bestowing,
In THARP'S FAMOUS BERKLEY RYE

THARP'S SONS
812 F [Street]

130

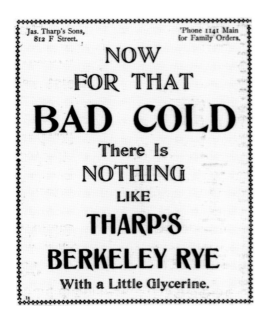

A James Tharp advertisement from the February 4, 1902 *Washington Times*, reproduced here. *Library of Congress.*

Finally, the following is an advertisement from the October 18, 1903 edition of the *Washington Times*:

Tharp's Nursery Rhymes

Little Jack Horner sat in a corner, eating his Christmas pie,
While Mammy and Pappy
Were feeling quite happy
Drinking PURE BERKELEY RYE.
Old Mother Hubbard went to the cupboard;
She wanted to feel quite sure
That the dog got a bone
While she sat alone
Imbibing THARP'S BERKELEY PURE RYE.
Jack Sprat could eat no fat.
His wife could eat no lean.
So, between them both, 'tis said
They licked the platter clean.
So happy this couple that
No medicine they'd buy,
For pain and ache they'd always take
A glass of BERKELEY RYE.

That story writ of Mary's Lamb,
A tale so often told;
To follow Mary where she went,
This lamb forsook his fold.
We wish the man who those lines
Would change his "pipe" and try
To tell the merits and the worth
of THARP'S famed BERKELEY RYE.

Sadly, within a few years, Walter's life and fate took a turn for the worse. On August 29, 1908, the *Washington Herald* ran the headline "Liquor Dealer Saved from Leap by Nurse Guards—Crazed Man Battles with Attendants on Fire Escape. Condition Is Serious." In the article, it was reported that Walter, identified as one of the best-known liquor dealers in Washington, D.C., after a weekslong stay at the emergency hospital, tore a heavy screen from a window on his third-floor room and climbed out on a fire escape. It took several orderlies to wrestle him down, after which, he was sent to the Washington Asylum Hospital.

14

WILLIAM J. DONOVAN

COLUMBIA CLUB

*W*illiam J. Donovan, in 1909, was the most popular Irishman in Washington, D.C., according to the *Washington Post*. Donovan had won a popularity contest run by the Ancient Order of Hibernians with a total of 3,849 votes, far outdoing the next runner-up, who received 2,035 votes. The order was an Irish American Catholic men's fraternity that sought to aid newly arrived Irish immigrants both financially and socially. First prize was a diamond horseshoe stick pin.

Donovan went to extraordinary lengths to promote himself, his saloon and his "Columbia Club" rye whiskey, which was sold between 1894 and 1917. It was billed as "the whiskey that made Washington famous." His advertisements were not his only appearances in the local newspapers; they also carried stories of his marital woes and the ups and downs of the Senators/Nationals, of whom he was a stockholder. At the time of his death in 1932, he was a Mount Pleasant resident; in fact, it was reported that he died in his house at 1644 Hobart Street. He was also a member of the Shrine of the Sacred Heart Catholic Church, and his funeral was held there.

Donovan first appears in an 1891 *Washington Post* article titled "A Troublesome Question," in which it was reported that he was granted a liquor license for 1907 Twelfth Street Northwest before an act, penned by the temperance society that prohibited the sale of liquor within a one-mile radius of the Old Soldier's Home at 140 Rock Creek Church Road Northwest, went into effect. The act was signed into law by President Benjamin Harrison, and it also prohibited the sale of distilled spirits at all army posts. It's the same act that helped thwart the rebuilding of the Schuetzen Park.

SALOONS— NORTHWEST

WM J. DONOVAN,

PROPRIETOR OF

BASE BALL HOUSE.

Fine Old Wines and Whiskies,

COLUMBIA CLUB,

My Own Brand of Pure Old Rye.

1528 Seventh Street, Northwest,

WASHINGTON D. C.

WILLIAM J. DONOVAN.

—The well-known baseball man "away up Seventh street" told all his friends in Washington yesterday that Johnson would win his game, having every confidence in Johnson's ability.

—Any time you want real information about what's going to happen in baseball, come in and he'll talk it over with you.

WM. J. DONOVAN,

1528 Seventh Street N. W.

Above: A William J. Donovan Baseball House advertisement from the January 8, 1897 *Washington Bee*, reproduced here. *Library of Congress.*

Left: A William J. Donovan advertisement from the April 20, 1911 *Washington Herald*, reproduced here. *Library of Congress.*

The article concluded that "[t]he settlement of the question whether these [licenses] are affected by the act will be troublesome." There were no other mentions of him or a saloon functioning at that location in the newspaper, so that establishment may have never opened. In a September 1893 *Washington Post* article, Donovan's wife mentioned that "her husband does a lucrative business as a restaurant keeper at 1528 Seventh Street Northwest."

Donovan's wife, the former Catherine McGrath, made her first appearance in the newspapers in the September 26, 1893 *Washington Post* article "Kate Donovan Wants Alimony—She Can't Live with Her Husband, and Religion Forbids a Divorce." In bringing a bill in equity against her husband for separation and alimony on the ground of cruelty, she declared:

> *That her husband is addicted to the use of intoxicating liquors to excess and indulges in periodical and protracted sprees. At such times, he is violent and has repeatedly assaulted her, threatening her life with a loaded revolver.*

On December 9, 1893, it was reported that Donovan held one of seventy-eight liquor licenses that had been granted by the Excise Board. His license was for the Baseball House Saloon at 1528 Seventh Street northwest. Donovan's Baseball House was located near the Boundary Field Baseball Stadium, which would later become Griffith Stadium, and it was located on the site currently occupied by Howard University Hospital. Donovan was also a stockholder in Washington's baseball team, then known as the Senators.

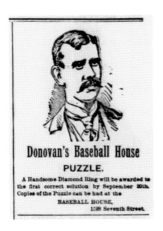

Donovan's Baseball House Puzzle from the June 3, 1894 *Washington Times*, reproduced here. *Library of Congress.*

THE BASEBALL HOUSE PUZZLE, 1894

In order to promote his new saloon, Donovan came up with a little campaign, the Baseball House Puzzle, introduced on May 28, 1894, in the *Washington Post*. In his first of many appearances in the *Washington Post*'s "About People You Know—What They Are Doing and What They Say," dated August 12, 1894, the puzzle says, "The Baseball House is well known to every baseball crank in the country, but Mr. Donovan's idea is to impress upon the public that the number of his popular resort is 1528, and his bright way of doing this is shown in the Baseball House Puzzle." Senator/Nationals fans were often referred to as "bugs" or "cranks" in the newspapers.

The Baseball House Puzzle

DIRECTIONS: Place and add figures 1, 2, 4, 5, 6, 7, 9, 10, and 11 in the nine circles so the total will be 1528, the number of the Baseball House. No figure to be used more than once.

The prize for the person sending in the first correct response was a "handsome diamond ring."

In the August 26, 1894 "About People You Know" column, we again find Donovan's visage with a short paragraph about the Baseball House that concludes, "Drop in Tuesday on your way to the big drill and make the acquaintance of one of the most prominent baseball men in the city."

The winner of the Baseball House puzzle was announced in the October 7, 1894 "About People You Know" column; his name was Mr. J.T. Hodgkin. The correct solution was revealed to be:

9	11	7
4	10	6
2	1	5
15	2	8

It was noted that:

Mr. Donovan remarked that he had taken a long chance in putting so much money into a puzzle, but at the time, he feels himself well repaid. It has made hundreds of new friends for the already popular Baseball House, and it will be a long time before Washingtonians forget that the number 1528 Seventh Street. Mr. Donovan has not fully decided but expects to soon offer the public another of these interesting contests, which demonstrates his very shrewd ideas of advertising.

Donovan next appeared in an August 9, 1895 *Washington Post* article titled "A Lecture to Liquor Dealers—Statistician Kammeron Presents a Strong Anti-Prohibition Argument." Donovan heard such arguments as:

A Donovan Columbia Club advertisement, December 17, 1899. *Library of Congress.*

Guiteau, the assassin, abhorred the use of alcohol but put a revolver to a bad use. Why is there not a universal outcry against the manufacturer of firearms? If a man makes a beast of himself in the use of liquor, why not punish him instead of attempting to deprive nine-tenths of the sober, temperate people of their means of enjoyment?

Charles J. Guiteau assassinated President James A. Garfield by shooting him in the back on July 2, 1881. For his crime, Guiteau was hanged in Washington, D.C., on June 30, 1882.

Above is an advertisement from the December 17, 1899 *Washington Post*; in it, Donovan touts the medicinal qualities of his Columbia Club. The text reads:

Many Families believe that a flask of whisky is one of the necessaries in a properly stocked medicine chest. Now, when you get that flask of whisky, be sure that it is the best. A recommendation here would have but little weight, but you will find that a large number of prominent physicians have stated over their signatures that nothing is superior to the brand "Columbia Club," sold exclusively by William J. Donovan, proprietor of the Baseball House 1512 Seventh Street. There are several imitations sold in the city, but the genuine article can be had only from Mr. Donovan.

"Mrs. Donovan Charges Cruelty" was the lede for May 27, 1897 *Washington Post* article in which it is stated that Donovan's wife, Kate, has now sued for a divorce, charging him with "repeated acts of violence." Apparently, they again reconciled, because here in the next lede featuring Kate, this time from September 9, 1899, "Mrs. Donovan Sues for Divorce—She Charges Her Husband with Cruelty, Drunkenness and Abuse." This time she declared:

That because of his violent conduct toward her, she has been compelled on several occasions to leave him, but upon his repentance and promises to treat her better, she had been induced to return to him.

Mrs. Donovan mentions numerous instances of her husband's conduct. While intoxicated himself, she says he frequently insists, in the presence of strangers and friends, that she is drunk and upon one occasion forced a policeman to arrest her and take her to a police station, where she was detained all night.

As we'll see, this isn't the last time that their marital bliss, or lack thereof, was played out in the courtroom.

COLUMBIA CLUB GOES TO WAR

The Philippine-American War took place between 1899 and 1902, and Donovan, like Tharp, used it as a current event to fashion his advertisements. In an advertisement made to look like an article from the March 4, 1900 edition of the *Washington Times* titled "'Columbia Club' at Manila" Donovan commented:

I have received numerous communications from Manila, letters from old patrons of mine, baseball boys who are still serving Uncle Sam in the

On Board The "Oregon," Watson's Flagship.

Even from the Orient—all the way from our new possessions at Manila—I have received several orders from our old-time baseball players for

Columbia Club Whisky.

Mr. Donovan has been long associated with the baseball players, many of whom are now serving their country at Manila. They speak very highly of the purity and excellence of Columbia Club Whisky, and attribute their general good health to a generous use of it. This flattering testimonial of my brand of pure Rye speaks for itself.

Headquarters for RARE OLD WINES and CHOICE CIGARS. Your trade solicited. We'll give you the best treatment and the finest goods in the market.

WILLIAM J. DONOVAN, Baseball House, 1528 Seventh St. N. W.

A Donovan's Columbia Club advertisement from the January 11, 1900 *Washington Times*, reproduced here. *Library of Congress.*

Orient. I have sent to them a pretty good supply of my own brand of whisky—"Columbia Club"—and recent letters from them tell me that they attribute their general good health to the use of this whisky in that trying climate.

As a part of the 1898 Treaty of Paris that ended the Spanish-American War, Spain ceded Guam, Puerto Rico and the Philippines to the United States. Apparently, the First Philippine Republic wasn't too keen about this situation and, led by revolutionary leader Emilio Aguinaldo, fought for independence rather than swap one colonial power for another. The battleship USS *Oregon*, known as the "bulldog of the navy," captured the nation's attention in the spring of 1898, when it raced nearly fifteen thousand miles in two months to get from San Francisco to Cuba to take part in the Spanish-American War, prompting the United States to push for the construction of a canal to make the transit faster. The USS *Oregon* was later sent to the Pacific to support the troops in the Philippines. Approximately 125,000 troops served in the Philippines during the war. After more than 4,000 Americans died and 2,900 were wounded, President Roosevelt declared an end to the insurrection on July 4, 1902. The American period in the Philippines didn't end, however, until July 4, 1946, when the United States formally recognized Philippine independence.

DONOVAN IN POLITICS

A curious article in the April 18, 1902 *Washington Post* reports that Donovan bought "a large tract of land in Alexandria County" and would shortly become a resident of Virginia. On account of taking an active interest in politics, "he desires to have a vote." At both the 1896 and 1900 Democratic nominating conventions, Donovan acted as a delegate, and according to his obituary, he got know two-time loser William Jennings Bryant well. It appears that Donovan needed to buy land in Virginia if he wanted a vote, because until 1961, when the Twenty-Third Amendment was adopted, Washington residents did not have a vote in the electoral college. Now, the District has the same number of electoral votes as the least-populous state in the election of the president and vice president. With a population of 714,153, according to the 2020 census, Washington, D.C., has more people than both Wyoming (581,075) and Vermont (623,251).

One District resident wrote a letter to the editor of the *Washington Post* in March 1900, complaining that "every obligation of citizenship to the government of the United States is strictly enforced against the people of the District, [but] they are denied the right of representation in the body which govern them." Even then, District residents mentioned the chant made famous during the American Revolution of "taxation without representation" in their vote-less plight. There was no further mention of Donovan either moving to or living in Virginia.

WASHINGTON POST'S "ABOUT PEOPLE YOU KNOW" COLUMN: WHAT THEY ARE DOING AND WHAT THEY SAY

Donovan appeared multiple times in this *Washington Post* column. Between 1901 and 1904, he appeared in it no less than seven times. Many were cursory references to how great both the Baseball House and his Columbia Club Whiskey were, but one really stands out. The August 23, 1903 section delves into Donovan's love of America's Cup yacht racing and the coincidence of the names of the two-time (1899 and 1901) winner *Columbia* and his Columbia Club:

> *The coincidence of the names will cause many people's thoughts to compare reliance of Mr. Donovan's Columbia Club Whisky with all challengers of the famous brand. Like the* Columbia *in her day and*

the Reliance *this year, it is the best of its class, the best purest whisky that money can buy, and its fame is almost as widespread as that of the beautiful yacht that is now battling for the supremacy of the seas. Many competitors have attempted to place other brands of whisky on the market that should have as much merit as Columbia Club and which could be sold at the same price of one dollar a quart, but they found it as difficult as Sir Thomas Lipton has found it to capture the America's Cup, and connoisseurs freely assert that Columbia Club is so much more superior to all other brands of one-dollar whisky that it is safe to carry the "broom at the masthead" for many a long year.*

The *Reliance* was the name of the 1903 American entry for the cup. Sir Thomas Lipton was the British skipper of Britain's entries: *Shamrock* (1899), *Shamrock II* (1901) and *Shamrock III* (1903). A well-used broom at the masthead has been symbol of naval victory since the seventeenth century, when Dutch admiral Martin Tromp was supposed to have lashed a broom to the masthead of his flagship to signify he had swept the British from the sea.

THE GOOD SHIP *COLUMBIA*

The nautical theme apparently appealed to Donovan, as evidenced by this advertisement from the January 26, 1907 *Washington Bee*, a weekly newspaper read primarily by Black readers during its run from 1884 to 1922.

HIDDEN ISLES OF THE SEA

Many a noble ship, laden with the proudest spoils of human industry and enterprise and freighted with that is dearer still—human life—has passed away with the morning sunlight glittering on its snowy canvas, passed away forever from the ken and knowledge of men as completely, as if it had never been in existence.

What has become of those vanished argosies? Whither have they gone? When the seas give up their dead and the old ocean lays bare its secrets, the human skeletons, the virgin gold, the priceless gems, the costly jewels and the wrecks of those vanished ships will be found strewn amid the tremendous passes and deep defiles of those submerged mountain ranges which are the backbones of lost continents, upon those topmost

A Columbia Club bottle drawing from the January 26, 1907 *Washington Bee*, reproduced here. *Library of Congress.*

peaks, projecting near the surface of the seas, these lost convoys have been dashed to destruction! The mariner's compass and the navigator's chart have not been able to protect commerce from the wreck and ruin of these submerged ridges, but the good ship Columbia, *richly laden with its precious "Columbia Club," the purest and best whiskey in the world, launched and navigated by William J. Donovan from the famous Baseball House, located at 1528 Seventh Street Northwest, with the Stars and Stripes glittering from its gaff and defiance to all competitors thundering from its steel-clad turrets, has weathered every gale and returned safely from every voyage, because Mr. Donovan knows the highways of successful enterprise are strewn with the derelicts of pretension and misrepresentation and that quality alone, and quality strictly and strenuously adhered to, is the only chart and surest recommendation of those who wish to indulge in the delicious, stimulating, health-giving virtue of a truly honest American whiskey—the "Columbia Club."*

MORE TROUBLE ON THE HOME FRONT

In another *Washington Post* article, it was Donovan who appeared unhappy and instituted a proceeding for divorce against Catherine, with the charges listed as "cruelty, violence of temper, habitual use of liquor and desertion." In his petition, Donovan provided some details of Kate's behavior:

> [Donovan] *alleges that the defendant assaulted him on many occasions and tried to seriously injure him and that about eight years ago, she entered* [Donovan's] *place of business when several customers were present and hurled bottles at* [Donovan], *breaking mirrors and causing him to close his establishment and seek personal safety; that three suits have been filed at different times by her against him for maintenance, but each have resulted in reconciliation, which has, it is said, as often proven a failure.*

Probably in conjunction with this filing, Donovan published this notice in the October 21, 1901 *Evening Star*: "Washington, D.C., October 21, 1901. I hereby notify the public that I will not be responsible for any more debts contracted by my wife, Catherine T. Donovan. Wm. J. Donovan 636 Q Street Northwest." This attempt at divorce must have also ended in a reconciliation, as we have one final *Washington Post* article about their marital issues in 1902, where its reported that Donovan filed an answer to a suit for divorce filed by Kate. In his answer, he states that Kate:

> *In the case, left him without cause, and that despite repeated efforts on his part to bring about a reconciliation, his wife refuses to live with him again. He states he knows of no cause for divorce and insists that there would be no trouble in their domestic life if* [Kate] *would cease using intoxicating liquors.*

We know that this suit also ended in a reconciliation, because in Donovan's 1932 obituary, Kate is listed as his surviving spouse. It seems that the love of strong drink may have been passed down to at least one of Donovan's children. A June 26, 1925 *Evening Star* article reported that twenty-eight-year-old Brian J. Donovan of 1644 Hobart Street "escaped death by drowning in the Potomac River at the foot of P Street Southwest last night. Unable to swim, he was saved by a man who passed nearby who heard his cries for help." According to the police, the younger Donovan had fallen into the river while wandering around intoxicated.

One of Donovan's daughters, Mary (also known as May), also made the news in a December 15, 1919 *Evening Star* article. It was reported that May, a resident of 1644 Hobart Street, at about 7:00 p.m. the previous night, was "knocked down at Columbia and Sixteenth Streets by an automobile driven by Miss Nellie Sweet of [the] Netherlands and slightly injured. She was taken home by Miss Sweet."

THE GREAT ENIGMA PUZZLE, 1904

Donovan's ran a second great advertising contest in the July 3, 1904 *Washington Post*:

> *William J. Donovan's Great "Enigma"*
> *An Intellectual Treat for Everybody*
> *Valuable FREE GIFTS for a Little Brain Work*

William J. Donovan, proprietor of the famous original Baseball House, 1528 Seventh Street Northwest, hits upon a novel and unique method to spread the name and fame of his world-renowned "COLUMBIA RYE WHISKEY," a brand that holds first place with all connoisseurs and judges for purity, age and flavor. Its name is known from Maine to California, and many a good "jorum" has been drunk in the far-off Philippines. Our soldier boys know its value in that trying climate and praise it as the highest tonic and finest stimulant upon the market. "COLUMBIA RYE" is Mr. Donovan's special brand, and he ought to feel proud of being sponsor to an article so highly recommended by physicians and lauded to the top-notch by those who have sipped of this pure nectar. In order to still further spread its name, Mr. Donovan has decided to give away, absolutely free, SIX full quart bottles of this famous rye to those who solve the sub-joined "Enigma."

Mr. Donovan's Unique Enigma

I'm seen in deep, but not in shallow.

I'm not in lead, but plain in follow.
I'm very plainly seen in note.
Also, I may be found in vote.

I'm not in mild, but in severe.
I'm not in month, but plain in year.
I'm not in earth, yet seen in ground.
And also very plain in sound.
I'm seen in Great Britain, across the sea;
In America, too, "Land of the Free."
In Russia, also, land of snow,
And Japanese, their mortal foe.
Our sympathy the Japs now share,

We hope they'll whip the Russian Bear.
I'm seen in Berlin every day.
In wicked Paris, too, so gay.
I'm next seen in Long Island Sound.
In Atlantic City, I am found.
Again, Chicago is my home,
And very plainly seen in Rome.
In Dublin and at Cork's fair town;
In Shandon Bells of world renown.
And that old land across the sea,
In Ireland, dear to you and me.
Put these letters together right,
And a well-known house will come to light.

Directions to Contestants: Pick out the letters from the names indicated—place them so that they will spell the name of the best-known house in Washington. The successful names will be announced in The Post *August 7, 1904.*

The answer to the puzzle was announced in the August 7, 1904 edition of the *Washington Post*. The three winners out of the 3,729 answers received were requested to call for their prizes at the Baseball House, with Donovan indicating, "I hope they take as much pleasure in drinking this whiskey as I do in presenting them with it." This is how the answer was presented—in a clever verse provided by the second-place winner (who was given two quarts of Columbia Rye Whiskey), Jack Ausmus of 17 Grant Place, Washington, D.C.:

In deep, I find the letter "D."
In follow, "O" is plain to see
"N" is the one I take from note.
And "O" bobs up again in vote.
Then from severe, take "V" away,
And add to it year's only "A."
The ground can spare its "N" doubtless,
And how would sound look with "S?"
Now, D-O-N-O-V-A-N,
And "S" to form possessive case;
A better name I "dinna ken"
Of any House or any race.
Great Britain furnishes a "B,"
So give us "A," "Land of the Free."
Then off to Russia for an "S."
She'd like to give us Japan (E's), I guess.
We'll "B" in old Berlin a day.
At Paris, stop and call for "A."
Then to Atlantic City bound,
First passing through Long Island Sound,
We find that each an "L" contains;
And now, it takes but little brains
To see the second word we spell:
"B-A-S-E-B-A-L-L."
"H" from Chicago, by the lake,
And "O" from Ancient Rome I take;
Also, a "U" from Dublin town
And "S" from Shandon Bells write down;
By robbing Ireland of her "E,"
We now have "HOUSE," word number three.
"DONOVAN'S BASEBALL HOUSE"

In all the country round.
'Mongst houses named
As widely famed,
It is the most renowned.
Fifteen hundred twenty-eight;
On Seventh Street Northwest;
Not hard to find,
If you're so inclined
To seek for what is best.
"Columbia Rye," the brand
Of Whiskey there dispensed
And he whose lips
This nectar sips,
Is richly recompensed.
Wherever glasses clink,
It is a favored draught:
Or East or West,
It is the best
That ever men have quaffed.

Donovan and the Senators

With a saloon named the Baseball House, it's no wonder that Donovan was a huge fan of the game. His obituary reads in part:

Donovan was instrumental in the formation of the American League Baseball Club in Washington and advocated the importation of Jimmie Manning from Kansas City as its manager. He was a stockholder in the new club and continued his interest in every phase of the sport long after he retired from business in 1917.

Baseball has been in Washington since the 1850s. The first record of the name "National" being used for a baseball team in Washington appeared in 1859, with the organization of the National Baseball Club by a group of baseball clerks who used to practice on the White House Ellipse. The city's first ballpark was located at Fifteenth and S Streets Northwest. In 1867, the Nationals went on a nine-game (they went 8–1) tour out west that did a lot to popularize the game. The following was written about it:

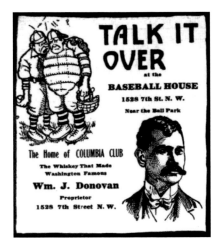

A William J. Donovan advertisement from the May 21, 1911 *Washington Times*, reproduced here. *Library of Congress.*

In 1867, the first extended tour of a professional baseball organization was made, the Nationals of Washington appearing in different cities of the Union, with such uniform success as to open the eyes of the people who had supposed the beauties of the game had received the fullest illustration at the hands of local amateur clubs.

There have been many leagues and teams in the city. The teams were variously named the Nationals, Olympics, Statesmen and Senators. Prior to 1903, across the country it was the Wild West as far as leagues went; they would come and go, some not even lasting a year. Players jumped from one league to the next and then back again, and there were numerous allegations of fixed games and league mismanagement.

THE AMERICAN LEAGUE COMES TO TOWN

Between 1892 and 1899, the Washington Senators (who were sometimes called the Nationals) played in the National League (which has been in continuous operation since its founding in 1876). The team had mediocre results, never finishing in the top five of the twelve teams in the league. Attendance at the games was not great, and whenever any player showed any modicum of talent, he was immediately sold to another team at a profit that was not reinvested into the team. The team played at a ballpark with wooden stands located at Seventh and Boundary Streets. Called Boundary Field, or simply the Boundary, it was located just outside the city limits (Boundary Street was renamed Florida Avenue in 1890). Donovan's Baseball House was located only a few blocks south on Seventh Street. The ballpark went through a few alternate names before it burned down in 1911 in a fire that was started by a plumber's torch. It was known as Nationals Park between 1892 and 1903, and then it became American League Park from 1904 to 1911. After the fire, it was replaced by a stadium built in the same location that would later be named Griffiths Stadium, which stood until 1965. If you go into the main entrance of Howard University Hospital and walk down the main hallway, past the elevators, you will find on the floor the exact place where home plate used to be in Griffith Stadium.

When the National League announced its decision to contract from twelve teams to eight, Washington, along with Baltimore, Cleveland and Louisville were left without a team, so there was no professional baseball in Washington in 1900. In January 1901, the American League was formed and sought to challenge the National League's dominance. It was formerly called the Western League and had been in operation since the early 1890s. The Washington Senators were one of the American League's eight original franchise teams. The other teams were the Boston Americans, which became the Red Sox in 1908; Chicago White Stockings, which became the White Sox in 1904; the original Baltimore Orioles, which folded in 1902 and was replaced by the New York team called the Highlanders, then the Americans and finally the Yankees in 1923; Cleveland Blues, which became the Indians in 1915; Detroit Tigers; Milwaukee Brewers, which became the St. Louis Browns in 1902 and then the Baltimore Orioles in 1954; and Philadelphia Athletics, which first became the Kansas City Athletics in 1955 and then the Oakland Athletics in 1968. The Senators became the Minnesota Twins in 1961. Starting in September 1900, the American League began to lure National League players to the new league by offering them substantially more than the National League's $2,400 salary cap. Washington was awarded an American League franchise on December 7, 1900. It was reported that the purchase price was $10,000. Donovan was part of the local group of investors who put money into the venture.

In a March 10, 1901 *Washington Post* article, it was reported that the Washington Baseball Club of the American League would be incorporated in the next few days, curiously enough, under the laws of West Virginia. One of the incorporators listed was James M. Manning. Manning was previously the owner and manager of the Western League team the Kansas City Blues. Manning was

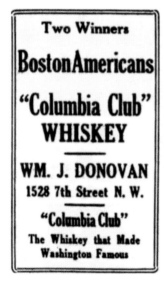

A William J. Donovan advertisement from the October 22, 1916 *Washington Times*, reproduced here. *Library of Congress.*

given an ownership share in the team as an enticement to make the move. Upon his arrival in Washington on December 17, 1900, he, along with other team officials, embarked on a search for a suitable spot for a new ballpark. The Boundary Field Park was not available, because the National League was angry that the upstart American League was bringing a team to Washington, and it leased the field to a local businessman who was supposed to set up a high-level minor league—but the funding dried up, and that league never started. So, Manning and his crew found a suitable spot a few miles to the east of Boundary Field at Thirteenth Street and Florida Avenue Northeast. They called their new park American League Park. The first formal meeting of the stockholders of the Washington Baseball Club was held on March 30, 1901.

Donovan was interviewed for a September 1, 1901 *Washington Post* piece on baseball:

> *In speaking of baseball, especially the Washington team, Mr. Donovan said that Manager Manning had the finest set of players in the American League and that it would not surprise him to see them in sixth place before the season was over. He considered Mercer one of the best pitchers that ever entered the box.*
>
> *Mr. Donovan says Manning is a hustler and a thorough baseball manager from beginning to end. He knows the players better than any man that ever was at the head of a team. Mr. Manning came here from Kansas City, where he was very successful in working up the best team that city ever had, and he certainly intends to do the same here by next season, as he already secured several leading players of the country for next season.*
>
> *Mr. William J. Donovan has long been known as a leader among baseball men of this city. He is very popular with the men of the different clubs and knows each one personally.*

The pitcher "Mercer" mentioned by Donovan was George Barclay "Win" Mercer. He had been a Senator for years until the league contracted, and he spent the 1900 season pitching for the National League's New York Giants. During spring training with the Senators, he made the paper in Phoebus, Virginia, and in Hampton Roads, Virginia (where the Senators did their training). Win was reported to have caught a runaway horse that was drawing four women guests of the Chamberlin Hotel at Old Point. As reported, "the speedy Mercer caught the team from behind and slowed it up until [teammate] 'Big Jack' O'Brien, the man mountain outfielder, made a flying tackle of the horse and averted tragedy."

It was noted that Win was a very handsome fellow who had a way with the ladies—so much so that on the days he pitched, usually Tuesdays and Fridays, such a large contingent of ladies came to the games that those days were branded "Ladies' Day" by the Senators. Unfortunately, just two years after Donovan's comments on Mercer, he was found dead by way of suicide. He was known to have bouts of depression, which he tried to cure by gambling. In the end, he found himself down some $8,000 and saw no way to pay it back. He left behind a note that said, "A word to friends: beware women and a game of chance."

It turns out that Donovan's low bar of a sixth-place finish was indeed met in 1901, but the season, it seems, had taken its toll on Manning as the manager. He had an ongoing issue with the team majority stockholder, Bryan Bancroft "Ban" Johnson, the person behind the creation of the American League who, in the early years, actually owned 51 percent of each of the eight original teams, over spending for the future of the team. Unable to work things out after one season, Manning packed his bags and went back to managing a team in Kansas City in a newly constituted Western League. In several newspaper articles, it was reported that all the local stockholders (presumably including Donovan) met with Manning to try to get him to stay. The following is from the November 1, 1901 *Washington Post*:

> While there have been attempts made by several of the local stockholders, whose aggregate holdings amount to less than one-fourth of the stock, to influence Mr. Manning to remain with the club, the efforts have not been made on account of any fear of the result should Mr. Manning sell out. Personally, Mr. Manning stands high with everyone connected with the club, and it was on this account that an effort was made to have him continue as manager of the club.

The new manager for the 1902 season was Tom Loftus. He had been poached from the National League's Chicago Cubs. But the major coup the Senators pulled off was getting Ed Delahanty to jump from the Nation League's Philadelphia A's. Known as "Big Ed" or "Del," Delahanty was a true (if fading) superstar in baseball.

The Sad Saga of Ed Delahanty

By the time he arrived in Washington at the age of thirty-three, Delahanty had experienced just about every type of on-field success possible. He was already destined for the Hall of Fame. He had led the A's in most offensive categories during his nine-year tenure there. Twice in his career, he made six hits in six times at bat and once hit four homeruns in a single game. He could hit for power, and he was fast. His off-field life was a different matter. His brief time with the Senators ended in what's been called baseball's most bizarre alcohol-related death. The following is a description of Delahanty from a book titled *Baseball Eccentrics*:

> *Men who met him had to admit he was a handsome fellow, although there was an air about him that indicated he was a roughneck at heart and no man to tamper with. He had the wide-eyed half-smiling ready for anything look that is characteristic of a certain type of Irishman. He had a towering impatience, too, and a taste for liquor and excitement.*
>
> *He liked to gamble—betting on horses was his thing. His much younger wife called him a binge drinker—once he started, he couldn't stop. He was an ugly drunk who was prone to violent mood swings.*

In 1891, he helped form a social club known as the Ancient Order of the Jabawauks, made up of some of his fellow baseball players, theatrical men and newspaper boys. The club's odd name may be a nod to Lewis Carroll's nonsense poem from 1871 "Jabberwocky" that was about a boy who fought and killed the dreaded serpent known as the Jabberwock. The following is an excerpt:

> *One, two! One, two! And through and through*
> *The vorpal blade went snicker-snack!*
> *He left it dead, and with its head,*
> *He went galumphing back.*
>
> *And hast thou slain the Jabberwock?*
> *Come to my arms, my beamish boy!*
> *O frabjous day! Callooh! Callay!*
> *He chortled in joy.*

The Jabawauks met every other Tuesday night to drink, sing songs and recite poems and essays. Delahanty even penned an essay called "The Ultimatum of the Usufruct."

Delahanty simply could not hold on to his money, and this is apparently one of the reasons he moved from the National League to the American League with the Senators, where he was offered a $4,000 contract with a $1,000 signing bonus (a significant increase on the capped $2,400 a year, plus an extra $600, paid under the table by the A's).

Delahanty was pretty much the only bright spot for the Senators' second season. He won the league's batting crown (with a mark of .376), making him the first and only person to lead both

ED DELAHANTY WAITING FOR ONE HE LIKES.

Ed Delahanty from the April 13, 1902 *Washington Times*, reproduced here. *Library of Congress.*

leagues in hitting (he did it for the A's with an average of .408 in 1899). But the team again finished sixth in the league. One curious aspect of the 1902 season was that whenever the Senators traveled to Philadelphia to play their American League rivals, the Philadelphia A's, Delahanty and his other teammates who had jumped from the A's to the Senators were unable to attend these games due to an April 22, 1902 Philadelphia Supreme Court injunction on players who had jumped from their National League contracts to play in the American League. These players were not allowed to play baseball in the state of Pennsylvania (unless it was for the A's) and risked arrest if they did so. The workaround was to simply avoid the state all together. When the Senators would take the train on a trip north to play the A's, the players who were subject to the court's ruling would jump off the train in Delaware and proceed to meet the team at their next destination after Philadelphia.

THE NATIONAL AGREEMENT SCREWS DELAHANTY

The Pennsylvania Supreme Court's ruling came at the height of the fight among the leagues over their failure to reach an agreement called the

National Agreement, which was the anticompetitive compact signed by all leagues, forcing them to abide by National League Contracts. After the 1902 season, the leagues reached an accord and signed a new National Agreement on January 12, 1903. Part of the deal between the leagues was that they had to allow players who had jumped their contracts by the time the deal was reached to remain with their new team. A committee was set up to decide the close cases.

Delahanty found himself in one of those close cases. Prior to the January 12 National Agreement, Delahanty had signed with the National League's New York Giants for a three-year, $18,000 contract, with a $4,000 bonus for skipping out on his Senators reserve clause. A reserve clause was a contractual device that owners could us to designate certain players as indispensable players that other teams could not negotiate with, basically locking certain players to a team in perpetuity. Prior to leaving Washington in the fall of 1902, Delahanty had, however, committed to come back to the Senators for the 1903 season for a $500 raise ($4,500) and a $600 advance on the season's salary.

With the Senators' money in his pocket, Delahanty made a beeline to the racetrack and lost every cent he had and then some. He wired the Senators' front office for more money and got another $1,000, which he also lost. Of course, during all of this, he was drinking heavily. It was at this time that Delahanty, way down on his luck, was found by the Giants (at a track in New York) and offered a big new contract. The $4,000 bonus was just enough to cover his loses at the track, and the three-year contract contained a very unusual clause that guaranteed he would be paid whether he played or not.

With the new National Agreement, however, Delahanty was ordered to remain with the Senators and to pay back the $4,000 advance the Giants had given him. Delahanty immediately wrote to Ban Johnson, the American League's president:

> *I don't intend to return a cent of that $4,000 advance money. My contract was a special one which provided for a certain sum a year, even if prevented from playing by injunction or disbarment.*

In response, Johnson made it clear: Delahanty's entire contract with the Giants was invalid, and the money had to be returned. Until almost opening day, there was a stand-off between Delahanty and the Senators, with a deal finally struck that said the team would pay back the advance to the Giants, and to take the sting out of the bite, they would take it out of Delahanty's salary over the next two years.

Delahanty showed up to training camp overweight and out of shape, and it was obvious that he had been hitting the bottle pretty hard. After putting in a less than spectacular performance for the first month of the season, Delahanty was sent by Manager Loftus to a health spa in Michigan to sweat off some of the pounds and get back in shape. Upon Delahanty's return in June, his numbers were better, but he was angry about being played in right field rather than his normal left field position. Prior to the Senators leaving on a road trip out west on June 17 for games in Cleveland and Detroit, Delahanty's life seemed to be spiraling. Before he left, he took out a life insurance policy on himself, naming his daughter Florence as the beneficiary. On the trip to Cleveland, he drank nonstop and talked on and on about how he would rather be playing for the Giants.

On June 25 in Cleveland, his hometown, Delahanty played the last game of his life. The next morning, after reading in the paper that the new National Agreement between the leagues may be in jeopardy and that its repeal would allow players to indeed jump from team to team, Delahanty went on a bender. It got so bad that he threatened to kill himself and some of his teammates with a knife. He slept it off and was assigned a teammate to make sure that he did not drink anymore during the double-header that closed out the Cleveland series. That failed, however, when he gave his assigned teammate the slip. He was so drunk by the time the team boarded the boat for the trip to Detroit that he barely made it.

Things were no better in Detroit. The Senators even went to the extraordinary length of having his mother and two of his brothers travel from Cleveland to try to get him on the right path. This gambit seemed to work. In the presence of his mother and a local priest, Delahanty signed a "be-good document," in which he pledged to treat Manager Loftus and the rest of his teammates "on square" and swore to "leave the 'red-eye' [whiskey] alone." His mother left Detroit on July 2. The moment she left, Delahanty found a bar and started drinking. One of his teammates tried to stop him, but he was chased off with a knife. Delahanty was despondent after learning that a court order from the previous day had extinguished any hope for players seeking to jump between the leagues.

When the rest of the Senators boarded the train back to the District, Delahanty was nowhere to be found. He had bolted for New York on board a train that was bound for Buffalo, via southern Ontario, and then New York City. According to all accounts, he was a nightmare passenger. After seven glasses of whiskey, numerous run-ins with the conductor (including one in which he brandished a razor) and annoying the other passengers

The International Railroad Bridge (1903). *Wikimedia Commons.*

around him, the final straw came when the train was slowing down to make a stop in Bridgeburg (now Fort Erie), Ontario, just on the other side of Niagara River from Buffalo, connected by the International Railway Bridge. Delahanty, drunk and disoriented, was trying to find his berth to get his luggage, as he thought that the train was pulling into Buffalo. He could not find his berth but did find a cabin in which a woman was sleeping. He proceeded to try to pull her out by her ankles. With the train now stopped, the conductor and two other men threw Delahanty off. It was around 10:00 p.m., and if he wanted to get to Buffalo, he was going to have to walk the last 3,600 feet over the bridge. The image on this page shows the bridge circa 1900–15, looking from the Canadian side.

What happened on the bridge and how Delahanty actually fell to his death remains a mystery. Bridgeburg's night watchman Sam Kingston, who was on the lookout for smugglers, supposedly encountered Delahanty, and in one of the many versions of the story Kingston told, he claimed that he thought that Delahanty was going to try to commit suicide, because he told Kingston that he planned to cross the bridge (which had no footpath) on foot. A scuffle ensued. Delahanty broke free and bolted across the bridge, into the night. The bridge, however, was open at the time to let a ship pass through, and Kingston claimed he next heard a "*splash.*"

Kingston's story seemed to change each time the Ontario Provincial Police questioned him. It turns out that he hadn't reported the incident until his shift change, many hours after it occurred. No one on the ship passing underneath had heard or seen anything either. Delahanty's body was found two days later on the American side of Niagara Falls. It had been swept over the falls and likely mangled by the propellers of the sightseeing boat the *Maid of the Mist.* The body was completely nude, except for a necktie and shoe, and one of its legs was missing. Delahanty's younger brother, Frank who was playing for the Syracuse team in the International League, was on the scene in hours. Frank immediately questioned how his brother's tie could still be in place, yet all his diamond rings be gone. It was also interesting that the same boat operator who had found Delahanty's body later found another body—this one belonging to a local farmer who had been carrying $1,500 in cash on his way home the day before he was found. Frank told reporters, "I have some suspicion about how Ed went off that bridge. The poor fellow is dead now, and he can never tell his side of the story, but the others can tell just what they please."

Delahanty's wife, Norine, filed a wrongful death suit against the railroad, seeking $20,000, and eventually won $5,000 ($3,000 for herself and $2,000 for Florence), but that amount was later reduced on appeal. In her suit, Norine alleged that Delahanty had $1,500 worth of diamonds on his person when he was thrown off the train. Delahanty was elected to the Hall of Fame by the Veteran's Committee in 1945.

NEW OWNERS, NEW NAME AND A NEW BALLPARK

The year 1904 brought many changes to the Senators. A new ownership group took charge, led by newspaperman Thomas C. Noyes, who was the city editor for the *Evening Star*, the paper owned by his family. His brother Frank B. Noyes, who was the treasurer for the paper, lived in Mount Pleasant's Ingleside Estate from 1896 to 1904 and was responsible for obtaining $200,000 from the Carnegie Foundation for the construction of the Mount Pleasant Library. Also, part of the ownership group was Henry L. West, who was appointed director. West was also, at the time, a District of Columbia commissioner, responsible for changing the street names in Mount Pleasant and all the suburbs outside the city limit.

With peace finally established between the leagues, the new owners were able to move the team back to the ballpark at Seventh Street and Georgia Avenue, now renamed American League Park. The 1904 season was a disaster; the club went 38–113 and were 55½ games out of first place—in the top five for the worst season record ever. The team's pitiful performance spawned the famous quip "Washington: first in war, first in peace and last in the American League," which appeared in the June 27, 1904 *Washington Post* and was credited to Charles Dryden.

In 1905, knowing the value of publicity, Tom Noyes sought to change the name of the team. The February 3, 1905 *Evening Star* announcement read:

New Nickname Wanted for the Washington Club
Season Ticket Offered for First Acceptable Title

The new owners of the Washington Baseball Club desire to get as far away as possible from the old regime and start the coming season without any barnacles to hinder its move toward prosperity. With this end in view, it is intended to bury the moss-covered title of "Senators" forever and a day and secure, if possible, another nickname for the team that may be lucky and consequently popular. To the first "fan" or "fanness" who may send a nickname to President Thomas C. Noyes, Evening Star *office, that will be accepted by the committee composed of the sports writers of* The Star, Post *and* Times, *a season ticket covering games at American League Park will be given.*

Some of the more interesting nickname suggestions came from a Sam Crane of the *New York Journal* and were posted in the February 10, 1905 *Evening Star*. Crane claimed that he wasn't "looking for the prize, but how would 'Tobaggans' do? Or 'R.R.R's—Railroad Rebaters,' or 'Interstate Commercers,' or 'Coming Chumps?'" In the end, most of the 2,305 suggestions were for the "Nationals," and the team nickname was changed.

The Miracle(s) of the 1912 Season

The Nationals' fortunes changed dramatically when Clark Griffiths took over the managing job in 1912. Accustomed to being bottom-dwellers in the standings, the Nationals put together a season in 1912 that, but for the Boston Red Sox, would have won them the pennant. The Nationals finished a distant second in the league, fourteen games out of first place, behind what was called "one of baseball's super teams," the Red Sox.

That year, though his team finished second, Donovan still found a way to have his own "miracle." It was reported in the October 17, 1912 *Washington Post* that Donovan won $5,000 off a bet on the Red Sox in game eight of the World Series (a 6–6 tie in the second game, which was called off by darkness after eleven innings, required an extra game between the Red Sox and the New York Giants to decide the championship).

The *Boston Globe* article from October 17, 1912, stated:

Words were never invented that could fully describe the outburst of insane enthusiasm that went thundering around Fenway Park yesterday afternoon as Steve Yerkes crossed the rubber with the winning run in the tenth inning. Men hugged each other, women became hysterical, youths threw their caps in the air, one man in the bleachers fell in a dead faint, strong hearts lost a beat and started off again double-time.

A picture of bottles found in the Mount Pleasant neighborhood. *Jason Hamacher.*

Donovan's heart probably lost a beat, given that the $5,000 he won on that day was almost enough to buy a house in Mount Pleasant at the time! In fact, he won more money than each of the Red Sox players got for the win (which was $4,024.68, according to the *Boston Globe* article).

Griffith went on to become an owner of the Nationals, and in 1923, the stadium where they played was renamed Griffith Stadium and was home to the team until it left town to become the Minnesota Twins in 1961.

EPILOGUE

There you have it, a sprawling snippet of both whiskey and Washington, D.C. history (that I hope you found as interesting to read as I did to write) bound together by a few whiskey producers who were working before 1917. Sifting through books, articles, blogs, obituaries, advertisements, newspaper articles, photographs, court cases, government and industry statistics, regulations, laws and artifacts has been great fun for me in learning about the life and times of these early whiskey men. Telling these stories for the first time and sometimes retelling them here has been enlightening.

The liquor scene today in Washington, D.C., is thriving—just as it was prior to when Prohibition came to town. The difference now is that we no longer import our distilled spirits from outside the city. We now make it right here! We now have a number of functioning distilleries within the city: Thrashers; Founding Spirits at Farmers and Distillers; the Ivy City Contingent; Republic Restoratives; Cotton and Reed; Don Ciccio and Figli; Alex Laufer's District Made Spirits (formerly known as One Eight Distilling); and the newcomer, Julia Fletcher's Bo and Ivy. My company, Reboot Beverages, hopes to work with each of these distilleries in the future as a "spirit architect," not just taking what has already been distilled and rectifying it, but getting involved at the beginning of the process to make spirits to our specifications.

Long gone are the crazy newspaper advertisements in which whiskey is claimed to cure every aliment, but there is a robust presence of D.C. liquors on every social media platform. A relic of Prohibition is the three-tier alcohol distribution system (still functioning in most states) that separates producers, distributors and retailers. (I would be remiss to not mention my two local bottle shops in my Mount Pleasant neighborhood that now sell "spiritous liquors": Arun Mody's Sportsman's Wine and Liquors and Jesse Chong's Irving Wine and Spirits.)

To ensure that the now-revived Mount Pleasant Club Whiskey brand survives into the next century, I'm putting a bottle of each of our batches (we are making a batch for every street in the neighborhood) in my attic's crawl space. By the time this book is published, there will be three batches up there (Nineteenth Street, Kilbourne Place Rye and Brown Street Bourbon). Only twenty or so more streets to go!

I wonder what the world will look like when they are discovered.

BIBLIOGRAPHY

American Telegraph. "The Sons of Temperance, Fourth of July 1851." July 3, 1851.

Ancient and Esoteric Order of the Jackalope. "French Leave, a Baseball Superstar, an Irate Owner, and a Clever Workaround." https://order-of-the-jackalope.com/french-leave/.

————. "Triple Jumper: The Mysterious Death of Baseball Superstar Ed Delahanty (1867–1903)." https://order-of-the-jackalope.com/triple-jumper/.

Baltimore Sun. "Announcing the opening of W.G. Bond, Inc." November 11, 1933.

Barton, Susannah Skiver. "In Whiskey, Age Isn't Everything." November 12, 2021. https://punchdrink.com/articles/bourbon-scotch-whiskey-age-isnt-everything/.

Bedford Weekly Mail. December 14, 1906.

Boston Globe. "Red Sox Beat Giants in 8th Game, Win World Series: Boston Now Supreme in Baseball World." October 17, 1912.

Bottled-in-Bond Act of 1897, United States Statutes at Large 29.

Boyd's Directory of the District of Columbia. Washington, D.C.: 1876, 1883, 1892, 1896, 1903, 1908.

Bready, James H. "Maryland Rye: A Whiskey the Nation Long Fancied—But Now Has Let Vanish." *Maryland Historical Magazine* 85, no. 4 (Winter 1990): 344–78.

Casway, J. *Ed Delahanty in the Emerald Age of Baseball*. South Bend, IN: University of Notre Dame Press, 2004.

Coffin, John P. *Washington Historical Sketches of the Capital City of Our Country*. Washington, D.C.: 1887.

Corrigan v. Buckley, 271 U.S. 323, 1926.

Cotter, Oliver. *Adulteration of Liquors with a Description of the Poisons Used in their Manufacture*. New York: A.S. Barnes and Co., 1874.

Cowdery, Chuck. "Let Me Rectify That for You." *Chuck Cowdery Blog*. November 23, 2015. http://chuckcowdery.blogspot.com/2015/11/let-me-rectify-that-for-you.html

Distillery Trail. "What Is Whiskey? The Taft Decision of 1909." August 24, 2021. https://www.distillerytrail.com/blog/what-is-whisky-the-taft-decision-of-1909/#:~:text=IMPORTANT%20ORDER%20IS%20ISSUED%20 BY%20PRESIDENT&text=26%20%5B1909%5D.,just%20what%20 they%20are%20getting.

E.H. Taylor, Jr., & Sons Co. v. Taylor, 124 KY. 173, 85 S.W. 1085, 1905.

Eidson, Bob. "The Taft Decision." February 17, 2014. https://www.gobourbon. com/the-taft-decision/.

Evening Star. "Another Division of Sons of Temperance." February 27, 1884.

————. "Application Denied." August 25, 1899.

————. "Barry, William D." August 27, 1936.

————. "Business Property Sold: Mr. Neligan Buys Building on 14th Street Near U." May 9, 1909.

————. "City Items." March 7, 1870.

————. "Danger of Fusel Oil: Dr. Wiley Contradicts the General Impression." February 10, 1906.

————. "Death of a Well-Know Citizen." December 3, 1889.

————. "Fifty Years Ago in the Star." September 29, 1929.

————. "His Final Decision: President Taft's Directions for Branding of Liquors." December 27, 1909.

————. "Installations S. of T." January 4, 1876.

————. "Joshing a Lady." May 21, 1910, 20.

————. "Karl Xander." October 2, 1897.

————. "Kept Their Own Secret." July 28, 1897.

————. "Kraemer Funeral Set for Tomorrow: Prominent District Resident Came Here in 1865-Retired From Liquor Business." June 10, 1932.

————. "Label on Whisky." October 18, 1907.

————. "Last Rites Sunday: Funeral Services Over Remains of Christian Xander." May 8, 1908.

————. "Lifetime Membership for Director Henry Xander: Washington Saengerbund Bestows Honor Upon Accepting Resignation." April 18, 1910.

————. "Liquor Licenses Granted: Action Today by the Excise Board Upon Applications Filed." December 5, 1898.

————. "Liquor Men Begin Their Conference: Committees Are Named at Opening Session in National Hotel." February 1, 1916.

————. "May Donovan." December 15, 1919, 13.

————. "Mrs. Delahanty Loses." July 6, 1905.

————. "Nicknames from Sam Crane." February 10, 1905, 9.

————. "Night Court Session for Celbrators Canceled: Few Cases This Morning Convinces Authorities Need Tonight Is Unnecessary." October 31, 1917.

————. "Notice to the Public." September 23, 1871.

————. "Paid $12 a Foot: Reported Price of an Uptown Building Site." June 10, 1906.

————. "Painter Near to Death.: Brain J. Donovan Rescued From River by Passerby." June 26, 1925.

————. "Pass Pure Food Bill: Vote on This Important Measure 240 to 117." June 24, 1906.

———. P.F. Neligan advertisement. March 17, 1913.

———. "Prepare to Fight on Liquor Control: Mt. Pleasant Citizens Appoint Committee to Secure New Members." December 10, 1933.

———. "Prize Winning Jingles." December 1, 1907.

———. "Prohibition Big Step For D.C., Says Author: Sen. Sheppard Declars Civilization and Happiness will be Advanced." Ocobter 31, 1917, 11.

———. "The Pure Food Law—A Magnificent Victory." November 30, 1910.

———. "Pure Whiskey: The Term Pure Whiskey Is Properly Understood by the Public to Mean a Whiskey Which Is Free from Impurities." March 5, 1906.

———. "Real Estate Transfers." March 18, 1901.

———. "Shoe Only Clew." October 10, 1909.

———. "Son Conducts Funeral of Patrick F. Neligan." October 18, 1934.

———. "Sports of All Sorts: American and National Leagues Declare Peace." January 12, 1903, 9.

———. "Sports of All Sorts: New Nickname Wanted for the Washington Club." February 3, 1905.

———. "The Temperance Campaign." September 29, 1883.

———. "Temperance Matters." November 13, 1876, 4.

———. "Thayer Is Named for Excise Board: District Temperance Workers' Slate Is Now Almost Complete." March 23, 1913.

———. "Want This to Be a Dry Town: Steps to Bring About Prohibition in the District." September 20, 1907.

———. "West End Division, Sons of Temperance." July 2, 1879.

———. "Where to Buy Groceries." April 5, 1912.

———. "Whisky and Quinine: Herman George Gets Thirty Days for Assualt." December 31, 1907.

———. "William D. Barry Dies Here at 72." August 28, 1936.

———. "W.J. Donovan Dies Suddenly at Home: Famous Baseball Fan and Harness Racing Enthusiast Was Widely Known." October 10, 1932.

Executive Order 1061. "Ordering Solicitor General to Report to President Branding Requirements for Whisky." April 8, 1909

Fair Housing Act of 1968. Title VIII of the Civil Rights Act of 1968 (Fair Housing Act), 42. U.S.C. §§ 3601-19, 82 *Stat.* 73.

Farrell v. United States, 99 U.S. 221, 1878.

Fleischman, Joseph. *The Art of Blending and Compounding Liquors and Wines.* New York: Dick and Fitzgerald Publishers, 1885.

Fogelsonger, M.I. *The Secrets of the Liquor Merchant Revealed.* Washington, D.C.: M. Green & Bros., 1933.

Geer, Emily Apt. "Lucy Webb Hayes and Her Influence Upon Her Era." Rutherford B. Hayes Presidential Library and Museum. https://rbhayes.org/hayes/lucy-webb-and-her-influence-upon-her-era.

Ghosts of DC. "Donovan's Baseball House: Finest Bar in the Country." January 13, 2014. https://ghostsofdc.org/2014/01/13/donovans-baseball-house-finest-bar-country/.

Grady v. Garland, 89 F.2d 817 (D.C. Cir. 1937).

High, Jack, and Clayton A. Coppin. "Wiley and the Whiskey Industry: Strategic Behavior in the Passage of the Pure Food Act." *Business History Review* 62, no. 2 (Summer 1988): 286–309.

In the Spirit of the Law. "A Brief History of 'Bottled in Bond." https://inthespiritofthelaw.com/2019/06/26/bottled-in-bond/.

Jackson, Cherese. "Is Whiskey the Secret to Long Life?" *Liberty Voice*, February 9, 2018. https://guardianlv.com/2018/02/whiskey-secret-long-life/.

Janvier, Meredith. *Baltimore in the Eighties and Nineties*. Baltimore, MD: H.G. Roebuck and Son, 1933.

Kurzius, R. "Is It Meridian Hill Park or Malcolm X Park? Your Answer Is Meaningful." *Washington Post*, Novemeber 5, 2018.

Lacour, Pierre. *The Manufacture of Liquors, Wines, and Cordials, Without the Aid of Distilling*. New York: Dick and Fitzgerald, New York, 1863.

Lee, Bill. *Baseball Eccentrics: A Definitive Look at the Most Entertaining, Outrageous, and Unforgettable Characters in the Game*. Chicago: Triumph Books, 2007.

Lewis, Carol. "The 'Poison Squad' and the Advent of Food and Drug Regulation." *FDA Consumer*, November–December 2002, 36. https://www.proquest.com/magazines/poison-squad-advent-food-drug- regulation/docview/220148588/se-2?accountid=46320.

Lindsey, Bill. "Historic Glass Bottle Identification and Information Website." Society for Historical Archaeology and Bureau of Land Management. http://www.sho.org/bottle/index.htm.

Maryland Distillers Guild. "What Is Maryland Rye?" December 11, 2017. An excerpt from Wright, T.W. "Chesapeake Rye—The Renaissance of Maryland Whiskey." https://marylandspirits.org/what-is-maryland-rye/.

McGuire v. Gerstley, 204 U.S. 489, 1907.

McLaughlin, D. "The Trubulent History of Rye Whiskey: The Real American Spirit." Cool Material. https://coolmaterial.com/food-drink/history-of-rye-whiskey/#:~:text=Rye%20whiskey%20was%20so%20ingrained%20in%20the%20American,measurements%2C%20George%20Washington%20was%20a%20veritable%20whiskey%20tycoon.

Modan, G. *Turf Wars: Discourse, Diversity and the Politics of Place*. Malden, MA: Blackwell Publishing, 2007.

Mount Pleasant, D.C. Citizens. *Mount Pleasant, District of Columbia, Centennial Celebration of the Fourth of July, 1876, with Annals*. Washington, D.C.: O.H. Reed Printer, 1876.

National Committee on Segregation in Nation's Capital. Text by Kenesaw M. Landis, Graphics by Tom P. Barrett. *Segregation in Washington, a Report*. Chicago: November 1948.

Official Gazette of the United States Patent and Trademark Office. February 5, 1935.

Ohio State University. "Medicinal Alcohol, Temperance & Prohibition." https://prohibition.osu.edu/american-prohibition-1920/medicinal-alcohol.

Olszewski, Ray. "Wine Made from Manassas Grapes Wins a Bronze Medal at the 1900 Paris Exposition: Who Knew?" *Prince William Reliquary* 8, no. 4. (October 2009): 73–82.

Packard, Aaron. "Washington DC's Schuetzen Park & Its Token." *Nova Numismatics*, April 27, 2022.

Phillips, John. "Fate's Beanballs" *Washinton Post*, January 7, 1990

Pickerell, D. "A History of the United States Seen Through the Eyes of Rye Whiskey, The Rise and Fall and Rise of Rye." Distilled Spirits. https://www.distilledspirits.org/wp-content/uploads/2018/09/The-Rise-and-Fall-of-Craft-Whiskey.pdf.

Pure Food and Drug Act of 1906. United States Statues at Large 34. U.S. Stats. 768.

Regan, Gary, and Mardee Haidin Regan. *The Book of Bourbon: And Other Fine American Whiskeys*. Boston: Houghton Mifflin, 1995.

Report of the Special Committee of the United States Senate on the Conduct of the Excise Board of the District of Columbia. March 4, 1915.

Rorabaugh, W.J. *The Alcoholic Republic: An American Tradition*. New York: Oxford University Press, 1979.

Saccoman, John. "Ed Delahanty." Society for American Baseball Research. https://sabr.org/bioproj/person/ed-delahanty/.

Schaller, Susanna F. *Business Improvement Districts and the Contradiction of Placemaking: BID Urbanism in Washington, D.C.* Athens: University of Georgia Press, July 15, 2019.

Sharp, Andrew. "Washington Senators I Team Ownership History." Society for American Baseball Research. https://sabr.org/bioproj/topic/washington-senators-i-team-ownership-history/.

Shelley v. Kraemer, 334 U.S. 1, 1928.

Slauson, Allan B. *A History of the City of Washington: It's Men and Institutions*. Washington, D.C.: Washington Post Company, 1903.

Sowell, Mike. *The Mysterious Death of Hall-of-Fame Be Ed Delahanty July 2, 1903*. New York: Macmillan Publishing Co., 1992.

St. Louis Globe-Democrat. December 26, 1882.

Stowell, Mark. *An Exposition of the Secret Order of the Sons of Temperance with Facts in relation to Secret Societies, Generally*. West Brookfield, MA: Cooke and Chapin, 1848.

Sullivan, Jack. "Christian and the Xanders: Selling Spirits in Washington, D.C." Those Pre-Pro Whiskey Men. January 15, 2015. https://pre-prowhiskeymen.blogspot.com/2015/01/christian-and-xanders-selling-spirits.html.

———. "The Muehleisens of Washington, D.C., Knew Liquid Assets." Those Pre-Pro Whiskey Men. October 28, 2016. https://pre-prowhiskeymen.blogspot.com/2016/10/the-muehleisens-of-washington-dc-knew.html.

———. "Phil. G. Kelly: Value in the Name." *Potomac Pontil*, June–July 2017.

———. "Whiskey Built Charles Kraemer a DC Mansion on a Hill." Those Pre-Pro Whiskey Men. August 14, 2014. http://pre-prowhiskeymen.blogspot.com/2014/08/whiskey-built-charles-kraemer-dc.html.

Thornley, Stew. "October 16, 1912: Red Sox Take Advantage of Snodgrass's Muff to Win the World Series." Society for American Baseball Research. https://sabr.org/gamesproj/game/october-16-1912-red-sox-take-advantage-of-snodgrasss-muff/.

A Treatise on the Manufacture, Imitation, Adulteration, and Reduction. Philadelphia: Published for the author, 1860.

United States v. Four Barrels of Liquid Purporting to Be Whisky, case no. 790. District of Columbia, March 13, 1909.

United States v. Ten Cases of Quinine-Whisky, case no. 10142. Northern District of Illinois, November 20, 1909.

Upper Valley Whiskey Society. "Distiller? Rectifier? What's the Difference?" October 24, 2019. https://uppervalleywhiskysociety.org/4648-2/#:~:text=Distillation%20versus%20Rectification&text=This%20process%20occurs%20in%20the,its%20flavors%20and%20aromatic%20compounds.

Urban, Raymond, and Richard Mancke. "Federal Regulation of Whiskey Labelling from the Repeal of Prohibition to the Present." *Journal of Law & Economics* 15, no. 2 (October 1972): 411–26. https://www.jstor.org/stable/724801.

U.S. Department of the Treasury. *The Beverage Alcohol Manual (BAM), A Practical Guide.* Washington, D.C.: Alcohol and Tabacco Tax and Trade Bureau, 2007, TTB P 5110.7.

———. *Occupational Taxes on the Alcohol Industry Should Be Repealed.* Washington, D.C.: Bureau of Alcohol, Tobacco and Firearms, 1976.

U.S. General Accounting Office. Alcohol Special Occupation Taxes. Washington, D.C. GAO/GGD-98-156, 1998.

U.S. Patent Office. Trademark 323,292. Registered April 9, 1935.

Van Orden, Chris. "No Beers for Years in DC." DC Beer. February 28, 2012. https://dcbeer.com/2012/02/28/no-beers-for-years-in-dc/.

Veach, Michael R. "The Fight for Bottled-in-Bond" Bourbon Veach. www.bourbonveach.com.

———. "History of Rectifiers or 'Non-Distilling Producers.'" Bourbon Veach. May 16, 2016. www.bourbonveach.com.

W.A. Gaines & Co. v. Turner-Looker Co., 204 F. 553 (Sixth Circuit 1913).

Washington Bee. "Hidden Isles of the Sea." January 26, 1907.

Washington, D.C. with Its Points of Interest, Illustrated. New York: Mercantile Company, 1894.

Washington Herald. "Lawyers Quarrel at Hearing." December 5, 1914.

Washington Post. "About People You Know: What They Are Doing and What They Say." March 22, 1903.

———. "Adopts 'Bone Dry' Act." February 22, 1917.

———. "Another Doubt Raised: Dr. Wiley's Statement About Scotch Whisky Sets Consumers to Thinking." September 24, 1904.

———. "Answer Filed in Divorce Suit." April 2, 1902.

———. "Ask License Transfers: Excise Board Hears Fice Applicants Who Would Change Permits." July 25, 1914.

———. "Ask Liquor License Changes: H.A. Seabridge and Charles Kraemer Want Their Permits Transferred." July 1, 1914.

———. "The Baseball House." August 12, 1894.

———. "Baseball House." May 4, 1902.

———. "Capital Pair Gets License in Virginia: Spencer B. Curry to Marry Miss Lillian Kraemer Next Thursday." February 1, 1931.

———. "Catholics and Secret Socities." March 1, 1896.

———. "Charles Kraemer." March 26, 1885.

———. "City Bulletins, To Cure A Cold." May 14, 1905.

———. "Columbia Club." April 14, 1901.

———. "D.C. Dry at Midnight: Senator Sheppard Here to Witness Wake of 'Demon Rum.'" October 31, 1917.

———. "Distillers Hard Hit: Must Label Blended Product 'Imitation Whiskey.'" February 24, 1909.

———. "Donovan Funeral Is Being Arranged." October 11, 1932.

———. "Dr. Wiley on Whisky: Chief Chemist of Agricultural Department Sends Views to Dealers." October 25, 1906.

———. "Elected by Liquor Dealers: William D. Barry Is Chosen President of the District Retail Assoication." October 29, 1915.

———. "Federal Seal Whiskey Advertisement." December 24, 1905.

———. "Five Were Rejected: The Excise Board Acts Favorably in Seventy-eight Cases." December 9, 1893.

———. "Furfurol to Blame: This Harmful Agent Is Not to Be Found in Really Old Whiskey." August 14, 1901.

———. "George W. Harvey." September 1, 1901.

———. "Grain Whisky Basis: Distillers of Other Substances Not Entitled to Name." June 8, 1909.

———. "Installation of Temperance Divisions." July 7, 1893.

———. "J.T. Hodgkin." October 7, 1894.

———. "Kate Donovan Wants Alimony: She Can't Live with Her Husband and Religion Forbids a Divorce." September 26, 1893.

———. "Kraemer Sole Distributor." January 31, 1904.

———. "A Lecture to Liquor Dealers: Statistician Kammeron Presents a Strong Anti-Prohibition Argument." August 9, 1895.

———. "Liquor Parley Vain: Bonaparte Ends Effort to Get Pure Food Definition." November 3, 1907.

———. "Liquor Squad This Time: Dr. Wiley Would Try Effect of Alcohol on Human Stomach." October 17, 1906.

———. "The Mount Pleasant Miracle: How One D.C. Neighborhood Quietly Became a National Model for Resisting Gentrification." January 25, 2021.

———. "Mr. Charles Kraemer on His Way to California." October 3, 1897.

———. "Mr. William J. Donovan." April 27, 1902.

———. "Mr. William J. Donovan." June 15, 1902.

———. "Mr. William J. Donovan Buys Property." April 18, 1902.

———. "Mrs. Donovan Charges Cruelty: Mrs. Grave Also Seeks a Divorce on Similar Grounds." May 27, 1897.

———. "Mrs. Donovan Sues for Divorce: She Charges Her Husband with Cruelty, Drunkenness and Abuse." September 9, 1899.

———. "An Old Order Revived." April 1, 1896.

———. "Presented to the Winner." October 2, 1894.

———. "Prof. Wiley Denies Everything." January 26, 1905.

———. "Prof. Wiley on Drinks: Shows House Committee How Whisky Is Made." February 28, 1906.

———. "Prohibition for District: Representative Webber Tells W.C.T.U. His Bill Has Chance." January 12, 1907.

———. "Pythians Are Especially Invited." August 26, 1894.

———. "Scotch Whisky." May 24, 1906.

———. "Scotch Whisky Bad: Dr. Wiley Files Report on Imported Spirits." October 7, 1905.

———. "Senator Magnates Organize." March 30, 1901.

———. "The Senators' Plan: First Game Will Probably Be Played Away from Home." March 10, 1901.

———. "A Significant Coincidence." August 23, 1903.

———. "Sons of Temperance Entertainment." March 21, 1894.

———. "Strikes at Secret Socity." December 31, 1894.

———. "Tell of Family Troubles: Five Suits for Divorce Instituted in District Courts Yesterday." October 25, 1901.

———. "Temperance Parade: Preparations for a Grand Turn-Out on the Twenty-Second." February 13, 1878.

———. "Thirsty Men Proclaim Willingness to Enter Wiley's Whisky Squad." October 28, 1906.

———. "A Tribute to Mrs. Hayes." May 2, 1878.

———. "A Troublesome Question." April 26, 1891.

———. "Understand Streets: Engineering Officials Elucidate Motive for Public." January 7, 1906.

———. "A Well-Known Man with Iron Nerve." June 12, 1904.

———. "Whisky That Is Not Whisky: American People Drinking Labels Instead of Real Thing, According to Dr. Wiley." May 18, 1913.

———. "White House a Winner!" August 7, 1904.

———. "William D. Barry Funeral Is Today." August 29, 1936.

———. "William J. Donovan's Great Enigma." July 3, 1904.

———. "Wins $5,000 on Sox: William Donovan Said to Have Wagered Heavily on Boston." October 17, 1912.

———. "Wives Refuse to Prosecute Husbands." October 13, 1904.

———. "W.J. Donovan Winner: Declard Most Popular Irishman in the City." September 26, 1909.

———. "A Word About One of the Fans." April 16, 1896.

Washington Times. "Anti-Saloon Body Demands Closing of Hundred Bars." March 13, 1915.

———. "Excise Board Gives Two More Licenses." December 10, 1914.

———. "Scientific Martyrdom of Poison Squad Over." May 24, 1904.

———. "Transfer for Liquor Licenses Are Filed." July 9, 1914.

———. "What Liquor Legislation the Needs and Why." May 13, 1912.

White House Historical Association. "Lucy Hayes, Temperance, and the Politics of the White House Dinner Table." https;//whitehousehistory.org/lucy-hayes-temperance-and-the-politics-of-the-white-house-dinner-table.

White, Philip S., and Ezra S. Ely. "Vindication of the Order of the Sons of Temperance Embracing its Origin, Nature, Design, Advantages and Progress." New York: Oliver and Brothers, 1848.

Wiley, Harvey W. *Beverages and Their Adulteration.* Philadelphia: P. Blakeiston's Son and Co., 1919.

———. "History of a Crime Against the Food Law." Doctor Yourself. http://www.doctoryourself.com/historyintro.html.

William J. Buttfield v. Nevada N Stranahan, 192 U.S. 470, 1904.

Wright, A.J. "Quinine With Whiskey: An Early American Drug Shortage." Anesthesiology News. October 20, 2019. https://www.anesthesiologynews.com/PRN-/Article/10-19/Quinine-With-Whiskey-An-Early-American-Drug-Shortage/56103?sub=39F3EE21EF6BE7E199A2177BB26557BBA01940DEAB525A3084AFDF9E76E4E&enl=true&dgid&utm_source=enl&utm_content=2&utm_campaign=20191021&utm_medium=button.

Yates, Freeman. *An Address on the Order of the Sons of Temperance.* Gardiner, ME: Weston and Palmer, 1849.

INDEX

A

Abner-Drury Brewery 112
Adams, John Quincy 88
Adams Morgan 89
Aguinaldo, Emilio 139
America's Cup 140
Ancient Order of Hibernians 133
Ancient Order of the Jabawauks 151
Anti-Saloon League 80, 81, 92, 93,
  94, 106
Appalachian Mountains 17

B

Barry, William D. 9, 13, 70, 73, 74, 79,
  82, 83, 85, 86, 88, 98
Baseball House 135, 136, 138, 140,
  142, 144, 145, 146, 147
Bell, Alexander H. 92
Bonaparte, Charles J. 48, 49, 50, 51,
  52, 54
Bottled-in-Bond Act of 1897 30
Boundary Field 135, 147, 149
Bowers, Lloyd 53, 54, 56, 57
Bryant, William Jennings 140

C

Canadian Club Whisky 31, 56
Capers, John 51
Carlisle, John G. 30
Carroll, Lewis 151
Caventou, Joseph 76
Cenlivre, Susanna 53
Chicago White Sox 51
Churchman, John W. 76
Civil War 17, 20, 27, 51, 76, 117,
  123, 126
Columbia Heights 85, 88, 108
Cosmos Club 48
Cotter, Oliver 25
court cases 21, 24, 31, 36
creosote 38

D

Delahanty, Ed 150, 151, 152, 153, 154,
  155, 156
Department of Agriculture 30, 40, 44,
  46, 51, 52, 106
Dockstader, Lew 35
Donovan, Catherine T. 13, 138, 142, 143

Donovan, William J. 133, 135, 136, 137, 138, 140, 141, 142, 143, 144, 145, 146, 147, 148, 149, 150, 157, 158
Drury, Patrick J. 112
Drury, Peter A. 112
Dryden, Charles 156
Dunlap, F.L. 51

E

Eckington 109
Excise Board 74, 82, 83, 90, 92, 93, 106, 114, 135

F

Fillmore, Millard 63
Fleischman, Joseph 26
Fletcher, George 16
Foster, John C. 68
Frank D. Reeves Center 70
fusel oil 25, 40

G

Gardiner, Edward L. 94
Garfield, James 128
Griffiths, Clark 157
Griffith Stadium 135, 148, 158
Guiteau, Charles J. 137

H

Hanna, Mark Alonzo 128
Harrison, Benjamin 133
Hayes, Lucy Webb 65, 66, 67
Hayes, Rutherford B. 128
Hayes, Willet M. 46
highway bridge 122
Hoover, Herbert 101
Hough, Warwick H. 36
House Committee on Interstate and Foreign Commerce 40
Howard University Hospital 135

I

International Machinists Building 125
International Railway Bridge 155

J

Janvier, Meredith 77
Johnson, Bryan Bancroft "Ban" 150
Johnson, Walter Perry 98, 100
Jones-Works excise liquor law 80

K

Kelly, Phil G. 90
Kennesaw Mountain, Battle of 51
Kingston, Sam 155
Kraemer, Charles 102, 103, 104, 106, 107, 110, 111, 167

L

Lacours, Pierre 26
Lamdin, Thompson and Co. 86
Lamont Park 107
Landis, Kenesaw M. 50
Leffman, Henry Dr. 28
Lipton, Sir Thomas 141
Liquor Squad 43, 45
Loeb, William, Jr. 48
Loftus, Tom 150, 154
Louisiana Purchase Centennial Exposition 36

M

Malcolm X Park 88
Manning, James M. 146, 148, 149, 150
McCabe, George P. 46
McGuire, James Charles 70, 96, 98, 100, 101, 107
McKinley, William 128
Mercer, George Barclay "Win" 149, 150
Meridian Hill Park 88
Monongahela 17, 20
Morris, John R. 70, 84, 85, 89, 90, 92, 93

Mount Olivet Cemetery 86, 101, 114
Mount Pleasant Citizens Association MPCA 102, 109, 110
Mount Pleasant Opera House 65
Mount Vernon Savings Bank 125
Mullowny, Alexander R. 85

N

National Agreement 152, 153, 154
Nationals (Washington, D.C.) 98, 100, 133, 136, 146, 147, 157
National Wholesale Liquor Dealers 36
Neligan, Patrick F. 73
Noyes, Frank B. 156
Noyes, Thomas C. 156

O

OKPB 85
Old Soldier's Home 124, 133
Overholt, A. and Co. 17

P

Park View 124
Pelletier, Pierre-Joseph 76
Philippine-American War 138
Poison Squad 34, 35
Prospect Hill Cemetery 125
Pure Food and Drug Act of 1906 30, 33, 36, 78, 101, 124
Pure Food Congress 36

R

racial restrictive covenant 107, 109
Red Sox 148, 157, 158
Reliable Family Liquor Store 70
Retail Liquor Dealers' Association of Washington 79
Revolutionary War 16, 19
Roosevelt, Theodore 33, 42, 48, 51, 52, 53, 54, 139
Rorabaugh, R.J. 74
Rosskam, Gerstley and Company 96
Russell, Hugh C. 107

S

Sacred Heart Catholic Church 101, 114, 133
Sangerbund 117
Sappington, John 76
Scharf, J. Thomas 18
Schuetzen 117, 123
Sheppard Bone Dry Act 83
Sheppard, Morris 84, 94
Shoemaker, A.E. 81, 92
Smith, Al 100
Sons of Temperance 58, 59, 60, 62, 63, 64, 65, 66, 67, 68, 169
Spanish-American War 139
Sprohs, Andrew 123
Stanley, Augustus Owsley 42
Stowell, Martin 60
St. Paul's Catholic Church 85
Strong, William 21

T

Taft, William H. 33, 53, 54, 56
Taylor, E.H., Jr. 24, 30
Tharp, James 126, 127, 129
Tharp, Walter 129
Tromp, Martin 141

U

United States Savings Bank 86

V

Vermillion, James O. 106
Virginia legislature 16

W

Walker, Hiram 33
War of 1812 20
Warren, Andrew W. 77
Washington Asylum Hospital 132
Washington Monument 63
Washington Senators (baseball) 147, 148
Whiskey Rebellion 19

Whisky Commission 51, 52
White House 54, 65, 66, 129, 169
Wiley, Harvey J. 30
Willard, Frances 66
Wilson, James 35, 46
Wilson, Woodrow 83

X

Xander, Christian 115
Xander, Henry 122
Xander, Jacob 119
Xander, Karl 120

Y

Young, Robert 107

ABOUT THE AUTHOR

Troy Hughes is a corporate attorney who has a side hustle of being a burgeoning whiskey producer. Based in the Mount Pleasant neighborhood of Washington, D.C., with his wife and kids (Isaac and Josephine), he spends his free time shuttling his kids from event to event, running or riding in Rock Creek Park and trying to come up with new ways to sell liquor. This is his first attempt at writing a book. A native of King George County, Virginia, and a graduate of the College of William and Mary and the Georgetown University Law Center, he proudly served as an air force JAG before settling in the District. More on him can be found at www.reboot-bev.com.

Visit us at
www.historypress.com